Shotokan Karate

Shotokan Karate
Its History and Evolution

Randall G. Hassell

EMPIRE Books
P.O. Box 491788, Los Angeles, CA 90049

www.empirebooks.net

Disclaimer
Please note that the author and publisher of this book are NOT RESPONSIBLE in any manner whatsoever for any injury that may result from practicing the techniques and/or following the instructions given within. Since the physical activities described herein may be too strenuous in nature for some readers to engage in safely, it is essential that a physician be consulted prior to training.

First published in 2007 by Empire Books
Copyright © 2007 by Randall G. Hassell

All rights reserved. No part of this publication may be reproduced or utilized in any form or by any means, electronic or mechanical, including photocopying, recording, or by any information storage and retrieval system, without prior written permission from Empire Books.

First edition
06 05 04 03 02 01 00 99 98 97 1 3 5 7 9 10 8 6 4 2

Printed in the United States of America.

Empire Books
P.O. Box 491788
Los Angeles, CA 90049
www.empirebooks.net

Library of Congress Cataloging-in-Publication Data

ISBN 13: 978-1-933901-28-2
ISBN 10: 1-933901-28-4

Hassell, Randall G.
  Shotokan karate : its history and evolution / by Randall Hassell. — 1st ed.
    p. cm.
  Previously published: rev. and ill. ed. St. Louis : Focus Publications, 1998.
  Includes index.
  ISBN 1-933901-28-4 (pbk. : alk. paper)
  1. Karate—History. 2. Large type books. I. Title.
  GV1114.3.H4 1998a
  796.815'309—dc22

2006010519

Acknowledgments

Having sought the advice and knowledge of literally hundreds of people in the course of writing this book, I find it impossible to list all their names here.

I particularly am indebted to Teruyuki Okazaki and the late Masatoshi Nakayama for their encouragement and support in the creation of the original edition of this book.

Special thanks are extended, for their encouragement and support, to John Corcoran, the late A. R. Allen, and the late Osamu Ozawa Shihan.

I hope the hundreds of others who helped and encouraged me will take the finished product as my thanks.

About the Author

Randall Hassell, Chief Instructor of the American Shotokan Karate Alliance (ASKA) and President of the American JKA Karate Association (AJKA), is a professional writer and editor who began karate training in 1960.

While majoring in English Literature at Washington University in St. Louis, he began an intense, formal study of the history and philosophy of the martial arts in general, and karate-do in particular.

To date, this study has led to the publication of more than 100 articles in numerous periodicals around the world, and more than two dozen books including *The Complete Idiot's Guide® to Karate* (with Edmond Otis), *The Karate Experience: A Way of Life; Conversations with the Master: Masatoshi Nakayama; The Karate Tournament Handbook; Karate Ideals; The Karate Spirit; Shotokan Karate: Its History and Evolution; Zen, Pen, and Sword: The Karate Experience; Karate Training Guide Volume 1: Foundations of Training; Karate Training Guide Volume 2: Kata—Heian, Tekki, Bassai Dai; Samurai Journey* (with Osamu Ozawa); and *Recognition* (a novel with Stan Schmidt).

In addition to teaching in his own dojos in the St. Louis, Missouri area, Mr. Hassell oversees the instruction of thousands of students in the ASKA, and he travels extensively, teaching, lecturing, and officiating.

Preface

When I published the first written history of Shotokan karate in 1984, I wrote in the foreword that it was the product of a magazine article that had gotten out of hand. I never dreamed that the book itself would get out of hand and have to be revised and expanded, but that is exactly what has happened.

Like any writer, I am delighted to see a continuing demand for something I have written, but I also have been mindful of the constructive criticisms of the readers.

I have been told again and again that the main thing missing from the original version was a description of the major and ongoing political travails of Shotokan karate. I can't deny, of course, that there have been political maneuverings and outright battles in the karate world (in all kinds of karate—not just Shotokan), but I have been reluctant to even discuss them with individuals, much less describe them in a book.

As I have thought about it, though, it has become clear to me that describing some of the major political actions of various organizations does not necessarily cast a bad light on either the organizations or their leaders. On the contrary, I think it helps to place the evolution of Shotokan karate in perspective—particularly in the human perspective, removed from myth and idols.

So I wrote down what I believe to be some of the major political difficulties the various organizations have suffered through, and as I look this book over, I am more sure than ever that 1) it is necessary to provide this information for historical perspective, and 2) describing such difficulties does not serve as an automatic indictment of the individuals involved.

In fact, I think all of the players in this drama end up looking pretty good because—and this is the critical point—none of them have turned their backs on karate. No matter how harshly any of us might judge them for their tactics, the fact remains that they have continued forward in their work for karate and that, it seems to me, compensates for a multitude of sins. It shows that, even if we disagree with the manner in which certain leaders did certain things, their intentions were at least pure enough to keep them on the karate path.

Since they are all still pursuing karate-do in their own way, they certainly don't need anyone's approval or disapproval to do what they have set out to do with their lives.

On balance, Shotokan karate is alive and well around the world and will be for many years to come. And it is healthy in no small measure because of the unswerving efforts of its leaders. Most of them have dedicated their entire lives to the cause of karate, and I, for one, am willing to believe that they have done what they believe to be in the best interest of their art. They deserve respect for their dedication, not vilification for a few individual actions.

Every chapter of this book has undergone major revision. In most cases, these revisions are expansions on the original work, and they include many significant organizations and important people outside of the Shotokan structure.

Many photos also have been added.

Also, any errors of fact here are mine alone. I have tried to present a balanced, unemotional rendering of facts. I sincerely do not wish to pass negative judgment on anyone in the vast karate world.

That said, I feel compelled to repeat what I said in the original edition of this book:

This work must stand as an exposition of my personal research, and in this regard, it must be seen as an unfinished work.

Those of us in karate-do know that mastery and understanding are fleeting: what we "master" and "understand" at our current level, we must approach again as beginners as we reach the next level. Such is the nature of our dynamic art.

Since karate-do is a very personal human endeavor, language is always inadequate. My desire is that readers with no experience in karate-do will make the effort to seek it out, and that readers with experience will be challenged to look deeper into themselves and their art, and to expand on this present volume.

Randall G. Hassell
St. Louis, Missouri
March, 2007

Contents

1: The Okinawan Roots 1
2: Gichin Funakoshi
   The Man and the Myth 21
3: Karate Comes to Japan 33
4: The Japan Karate Association
   Karate for the Rest of the World 53
5: Karate Comes to the United States 85
6: The JKA in the United States 123
7: Ideal and Reality 143

Epilogue: 164
Notes 167

Appendix A: The Origins of Shotokan Kata 169
Appendix B: The Basic 15 Kata of Shotokan
   and Their Technical Value 174
Appendix C: Genealogy of Modern Karate 177

Index 187

1
The Okinawan Roots

Modern karate-do had its origins on Okinawa, the largest island in a chain of more than 60 tiny islands south of the Japanese mainland, known as the Ryukyus. Okinawa is conveniently located for trade in the Pacific, lying 300 miles from the southern Japanese island of Kyushu, 375 miles from Taiwan, and only 500 miles from Foochow on the Chinese mainland.

Until the first century B.C., the Ryukyu islands exhibited a stone age culture. Farming implements and weapons were primitive and crude, and fighting "systems" as such did not exist. From the first through the 15th centuries, the Ryukyus were divided into three

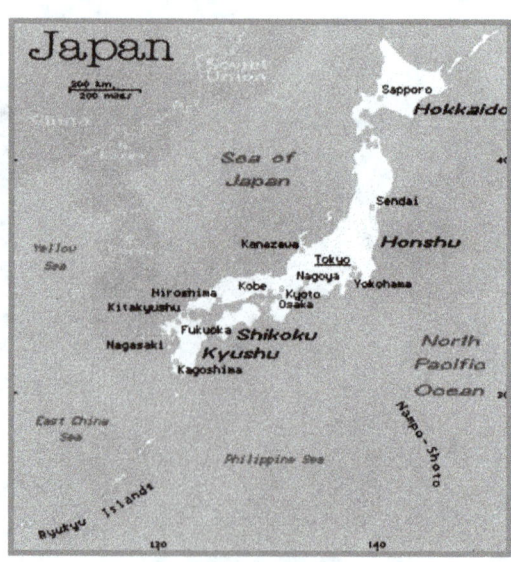

Yumi & ya (bow and arrow)

small kingdoms—Chuzan, Nanzan, and Hokuzan—and these kingdoms were dominated by numerous chieftains who placed high value on military expertise. During the seventh and eighth centuries, in particular, internal strife was more or less constant, with each chieftain vying for power and control.

In the 10th century, with the Taira and Minamoto clans waging heavy war in Japan, Okinawa became a refuge for many Japanese seeking to escape fomentation in the homeland. Many of these Japanese brought with them to Okinawa a number of fighting arts, weapons, and skills, and they were afforded much respect and honor by the Okinawans. During this period, the Okinawans were first introduced to the Japanese versions of bow and arrow *(yumi and ya)*, the spear *(yari)*, the halberd *(naginata)*, and swords *(katana* and *tachi).*

Since the Okinawans were by temperament a peace-loving people, it is not surprising that the first king of Okinawa, Shunten, placed high priority on military matters for the defense of his kingdom. Indeed, the hallmarks of his 13th century reign included the building of numerous castles and forts.

From about 1350, Okinawa steadily developed formal relations with China, Korea, and Japan proper. Because of the strategic placement of the islands in the East China Sea, Ryukyuans

The Okinawan Roots

enjoyed strong trade relationships with (in addition to China, Korea, and Japan), Java, Sumatra, Siam, Arabia, and Malacca. There can be no doubt that the influx of foreign traders, merchant marines, and seamen brought the Okinawans in touch with fighting arts indigenous to these various countries.

In 1429, the king of Chuzan, Sho Hashi, succeeded in uniting the three kingdoms into one, and in 1477, Sho Shin, the grandson of Sho Hashi, issued an edict banning the possession of weapons. This was done primarily to prevent would-be rulers from building up armies and fortifications.

In 1609, the Shimazu Clan, the rulers of the Satsuma Domain of Kyushu, conquered Okinawa and took steps to turn the island kingdom into a colony. Since both officials and commoners were prohibited from possessing weapons, the Shimazu had little trouble overwhelming the agrarian Okinawans. In fact, the peaceful Okinawans offered virtually no organized or effective resistance. To further bolster their rule, the Shimazu again issued an edict banning the possession of weapons. Even some farming implements were stored in government warehouses, where they could be checked out in the morning and returned before dark.

In 1669, even the manufacture of ceremonial swords was banned in Okinawa, and the Okinawans literally were left "empty-handed."

While there is some doubt about the effectiveness and enforcement of these weapons bans, there is little doubt that these successive bans on weapons helped to encourage Okinawan resentment against Shimazu rule, and that this resentment, coupled with resentment toward their own leaders in the 15th century, strongly influenced the development of empty-handed combat arts in the Ryukyu Islands.

Among modern karate-ka, there exists a commonly held belief that the Chinese taught the Okinawans Chinese fighting arts and that the Okinawans then transformed these arts into *te* ("hand") and eventually into karate. While not without merit, this simplistic historical view is somewhat less than accurate. In fact, it is highly unlikely that very many Chinese highly skilled in the courtly martial arts of their mainland spent enough time in Okinawa to transmit the depth of these arts to the Okinawans. There is also little likelihood that the Chinese, who considered themselves socially and culturally superior to the Okinawans, would spend much time teaching courtly arts in an organized or formal fashion to their "inferiors."

It is much more likely that the Okinawans developed *te* as an indigenous art of their culture, clearly influenced by the Chinese, Koreans, and Siamese, but largely structured from their own instincts and ideas.

Some proof of the originality of the Okinawans in developing *te* is offered by the observation that the Amami Islands were separated from Okinawa by the Shimazu, and even though these islands enjoyed essentially the same contact with the Chinese as did Okinawa proper, nothing resembling Okinawa-te developed there.

The primary physical influence of the Chinese on the development of Okinawan fighting systems probably arose around the settlement of Kumemura, a village near Naha. In 1392, 36 Chinese families established their homes there as part of the Ming Dynasty tradition of sending families to collect tribute from nearby countries with which the Chinese enjoyed trade relationships. As many as 500 Chinese could be found in Kumemura at any given moment, and the majority of these people remained there for only about six months at a time. In some cases, however, a few Chinese remained in Kumemura for several years at a time. Among these 36 families were a number of Zen Buddhists who taught their religion and philosophy to the Okinawans.

In the absence of a large body of written records, it is possible only to surmise the extent to which these Chinese attempted to teach Chinese martial arts to the Okinawans, but it can be assumed that, at the very least, they introduced a number of Okinawans to elements of various Chinese fighting arts. Some scholars today, for example, believe that the famous Chinese, Kung Siang Chun (Koshokun in Japanese), the man

The Okinawan Roots

credited with introducing the famous kata now known as Kanku to the Okinawans, was a Chinese envoy during the Ming dynasty, while others cite references to such a man as a shipwrecked sailor. Still another insists that Koshokun was a resident of the village of Kumemura for more than 10 years. While it appears certain that such a person existed, the written historical record leaves us with only one, indisputable fact: Regardless of how much Koshokun or any other Chinese taught the Okinawans about fighting, there can be no doubt that the Okinawans, who considered themselves to be of a lower caste than the Chinese, were enthralled with the philosophical foundations of the courtly Chinese martial arts, and they rushed to associate themselves with anything Chinese.

Also, it is clear that no matter how much of Chinese boxing was introduced to Okinawa, the Okinawans made vast changes in it and added their own, unique ideas and concepts to it. It is this uniquely Okinawan art that was the progenitor of modern karate-do.

In many ways, Okinawa-te developed according to the lifestyles of the people, and the techniques developed and employed are reflections of the varied lifestyles of the Okinawans.

Broadly speaking, the techniques of Okinawa-te can be considered in two categories: the techniques of the farmers and the techniques of the fishermen. In general, the farmers, who spent long hours squatting in the fields, planting, tending, and harvesting rice, tended to favor techniques supported by broad, low stances—techniques that relied heavily on defending oneself from a low or crouching position. Techniques developed around fishing villages, on the other hand, make extensive use of fast and strong movements of the arms—arms that had been strengthened by casting and retrieving nets. Little emphasis was placed on low stances in fishing villages.

Beginning in the 18th century, the development of karate became more open and, consequently, the deeds of the masters were more accurately recorded. The pivotal figure in the early development of the karate that ultimately produced Shotokan, was Sokon "Bushi" Matsumura (1796–1884).

Matsumura reportedly was raised (after his father's death, when Sokon was 3 years old) by "Tode" Sakugawa (1733–1815). Sakugawa was the most prominent exponent of fisticuffs of his time on Okinawa, and had himself been taught by Peichin Takahara (1683–1760). It is also believed that Sakugawa traveled to China frequently, for the specific purpose of furthering his boxing skills.

Legend aside, though, Matsumura (nicknamed "Bushi" or "warrior" by Sakugawa), produced the most highly skilled karate practitioners of the time. His two most influential students, who both later became the teachers of Gichin Funakoshi, the founder of Shotokan karate, were Yasutsune Itosu (1830–1915) and Yasutsune Azato (1827–1906).

Further, the Okinawans by no means limited themselves to empty-handed techniques. Indeed, they displayed great ingenuity in turning their farming and fishing implements into deadly weapons. Undoubtedly, the Okinawans began developing the use of farming and fishing implements as weapons even before they began systematically developing empty-hand techniques. What is today called *kobudo*, the arts of weaponry, was then called *te gua* ("hand implements"), and some of its exponents were very formidable fighters.

From the fisherman came two popular weapons that could be wielded with deadly accuracy and effect. The *nunte* and *sai*, both used as gaffs during the day, became deadly weapons in the hands of a *te gua* expert.

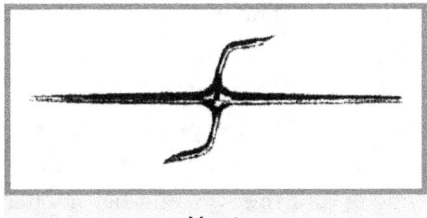

Nunte

The *nunte* was a cast iron implement about two feet long, about one inch thick in the center, and tapered to points on each

The Okinawan Roots

end, both for piercing effect and to provide balance. On each side of the *nunte* was a sharp tine, one pointing toward each end of the shaft.

The *nunte* could be used effectively against a swordsman by catching the blade of the sword in one of the tines and then jerking the sword away from the swordsman with a sharp snap of the wrist, or, in a more fluid motion, pinning the sword blade to the ground. Some fishermen carried two *nunte*, concealing one in their clothing or hanging it from their waist sash behind their back. In this fashion, one *nunte* could be used for parrying a sword stroke, and the other could be used to stab the opponent.

In some instances, the *nunte* would be tied to a long staff *(bo)*, and wielded like a spear or halberd. Used in this fashion, the *nunte* was extremely effective against armed warriors, for it gave the fisherman an important edge in distance from the swordsman.

A variation of the *nunte* was the *sai,* similar in construction, but with both tines pointing toward the sharpened end of the center shaft. The shaft also had one shorter, blunted end, which could be used to augment empty-handed techniques. The main advantage of the *sai* was that it could be held with

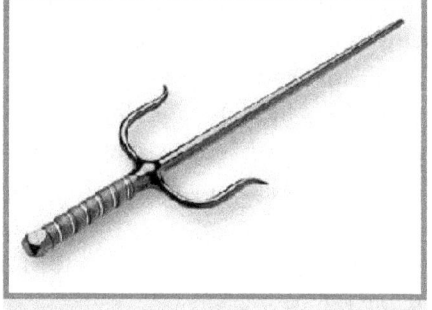

Sai

the pointed end lying along the forearm, and the blunted end extending outward from the hand. With a flip of the wrist, the long end of the *sai* could be snapped forward, catch a swordsman's blade, twist it away from him, and either stab him with the sharp end, strike him with a flipping action of the long shaft, or retrieve the long end and jab him with the short, blunt end. Further, the holding of the *sai* along the forearm enabled the fisherman to block or parry a sword stroke at close range with his iron-protected arm, and move in for the kill. Like the *nunte,* the *sai* was often carried in pairs, for the same reasons and with the same results.

The first thing most people think of when they see a *nunte* or *sai* is that it is a throwing weapon, but in reality, these weapons were rarely thrown, except as a last resort. Fishermen carrying three *sai* might throw one to distract the opponent, but both the *nunte* and *sai* were far more effective as handheld weapons than as projectiles.

Another contribution of the fishermen to *te gua* was the *eku,* or long oar.

Although a heavy and somewhat cumbersome weapon, the *eku* nevertheless could be used to great effect in sweeping the opponent off his feet, parrying blows from other weapons, and jabbing and striking. Comparatively little ingenuity was required to use the *eku* as a weapon, and as a formal system of weaponry, it is today almost extinct. In the hands of an Okinawan fisherman, however, the *eku* was a very effective weapon.

For all their ingenuity, Okinawan fishermen were overshadowed in the development of weapons by Okinawan farmers. Farmers had many more tools at their disposal than fishermen, and, consequently, they were able to develop a much larger arsenal than the fishermen.

While virtually all of the tools and implements turned into weapons by the Okinawans were in general use throughout Southeast Asia, it was the Okinawans who showed the greatest ingenuity in developing those implements into weapons.

Bo

The Okinawan Roots

One such weapon, the *bo*, was a nearly six-foot staff of hardwood that could be conveniently whittled from almost any tree or branch of sufficient size.

As a fighting instrument, the staff has been used since antiquity, and in fact, the Japanese martial arts recognized hundreds of different schools of *bo-jutsu*, or "arts of the staff." Almost all of the Japanese schools of *bo-jutsu*, however, utilized a thick, heavy rod of wood called *rokushaku*. The Okinawans, on the other hand, developed a thinner, lighter, tapered shaft for the *bo*, and this provided them with superior speed and flexibility in the application of their techniques. Of all the arts of Okinawan weaponry, the *bo* was probably the most highly developed and carefully studied. Kata from the various masters of the *bo* today number in the hundreds, and entire styles of *bo-jutsu* have been created in accord with the principles developed by the early Okinawans.

It is likely that the tapered *bo* was a natural outgrowth of the use of gaff handles and plow handles as staves. Whether by design or chance, the tapering of the *bo* into a lighter staff was of great importance in the development of Okinawan staff techniques, and it served the Okinawans well in combat.

In addition to the *bo,* farmers also made extensive use of the *kama* (a sickle), the *tonfa* (a handle from a rice grinder) and the *nunchaku* (a wooden flail).

Of these three weapons, the *kama* was probably the most effective and versatile.

The sharpened, curved blade was attached perpendicular to a short, wooden handle.

Not only could this weapon be used to slash and cut, but it also could (much like the *sai)* be held along the forearm to protect the arm

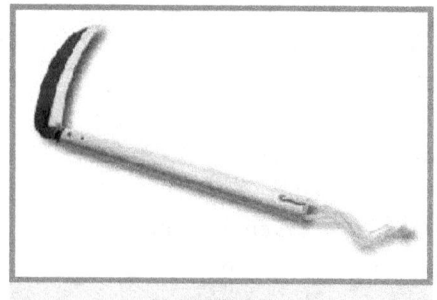

Kama

and then to whip out at an opponent. Two *kama,* one held in each hand, could be waved and whipped around the body and the head in a circular fashion, providing protection from a multitude of attacks from multiple opponents. This short *kama* (about two feet long) usually consisted of a wooden handle and an eight-inch or 10-inch, slightly curved blade, sharpened on one side.

A longer, sturdier version of the *kama* exhibited a straighter blade sharpened on both sides. This *kama* often was tied to a long pole and used in the fashion of the Japanese halberd *(naginata).* Not only was it an effective weapon at longer range, but it also proved very effective in slashing the legs of enemy horses.

Another variation was called *nichigama,* and it consisted of two short *kama* tied together by a long rope or piece of chain.

This enabled the farmer to throw one *kama,* ensnaring the opponent and drawing him close, and then hack him to pieces with the other blade. Another, more advanced technique involved throwing both blades at once while holding onto the center of the rope or chain. Used in this fashion, the *kama* would scissor past each other in the air and return to the sender in boomerang fashion. As might be imagined, this technique was at the apex of *kama* technique in terms of difficulty of execution and the degree of skill required of the user.

A *kama* attached at the end of the handle or the base of the blade to a long chain with a lead weight on the other end was called *kusarigama,* and could be used in bolo fashion to trip a man or horse, drag him near, and kill him with the blade.

The attachment of a chain or rope to a *kama* also made it possible to throw the weapon and retrieve it easily.

Kusarigama

As an instrument of versatility, the *tonfa* also ranks high among indigenous Okinawan weaponry. The *tonfa* was a square shaft of oak, about two feet long, with a four- or five-inch handle set perpendicular to the shaft, about five or six inches from one end.

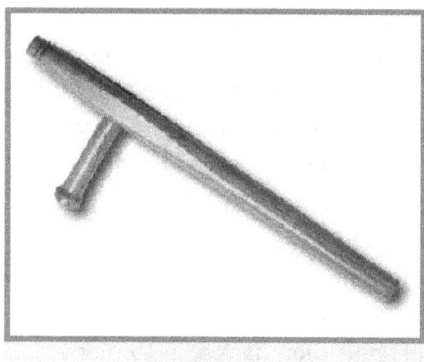

Tonfa

The *tonfa* was an integral part of the millstone used to grind rice, so it was a very common implement among farmers. The millstone used by the Okinawans consisted of a stone, which was rolled over the rice as it lay in a shallow groove. The *tonfa* was inserted in a hole cut in the grinding stone and was used to move the stone back and forth across the rice. Thus, it was easily removable, and the short handle could be grasped to turn the *tonfa* into an effective weapon.

A farmer holding a pair of *tonfa* could use one lying along his forearm to block or parry a blow, and since the ends of the weapon extended beyond both the fist and the elbow, he might use the other to jab, punch, or even strike with the end protruding past the elbow. By grasping the short handle in a light grip, the practitioner could also spin the long end of the *tonfa* toward an assailant, either tightening his grip to make a forceful strike, or letting the *tonfa* continue to spin in a raking motion across the opponent's face.

In close combat, the long end of the *tonfa* could be grasped, and the short, protruding handle used in grappling hook fashion to grab an opponent's knee and unbalance him.

Of all the weapons derived from *te gua*, the most popular today is the *nunchaku*, or flail.

Nunchaku

When harvesting rice, Okinawan farmers would cut the grain with a *kama* and then separate the grain from the chaff with a wooden flail. This flail, the *nunchaku*, was made of two tapered sticks of wood, each about one inch thick, connected at the tapered ends by braided horse hair, or sometimes by a thick, sturdy vine called *kanda*. In modern times, horse hair has been replaced by heavy cord or a length of chain.

A little-known fact in the Western world today is that there were many different kinds of *nunchaku*, and many of them had three *(san-kon nunchaku)* or four *(yon-setsu-kon nunchaku)* pieces. Neither were the pieces of the *nunchaku* all of uniform length. *So-setsu-kon nunchaku* was composed of one section only one-half the length of the other, and *san-setsu-kon nunchaku* displayed one piece of normal length attached to two smaller pieces. Some *nunchaku* were octagonal in shape *(hakakukei nunchaku)*, some were round *(marugata nunchaku)*, and still others were only half-round *(han-kei nunchaku)*.

But no matter what shape or form the *nunchaku* took, it proved to be a very deadly weapon in the hands of a skilled practitioner. Holding one end firmly, the wielder of the *nunchaku* could generate tremendous force in the other end of the instrument by swinging it in deadly patterns at his assailant. Particularly effective in disarming an opponent, the sticks of the *nunchaku* could also be grasped, either singly or together, and used as a cudgel or truncheon at close range. Other effective close range uses of the *nunchaku* included the use of it as a garrote for strangling the opponent and as a pincer against the limbs or head.

Since the *nunchaku* was easily concealed in a person's clothing,

The Okinawan Roots

and since it could be used effectively even by those with limited skills, it quickly became the most popular weapon among the Okinawan peasants.

Since possession of weaponry was prohibited, *te gua* experts had to practice in secrecy, and their skills were passed on to others by word of mouth and in the form of kata containing the techniques and movements of each expert's individual style. Many of these kata are still practiced today.

Other weapons, in addition to the primary ones mentioned above, were used by the Okinawans, but their use was never systematized or passed along from generation to generation in as formal a manner as the others. These included, among others, the *suruchin* (a rope weighted at both ends and used as a bolo), the *kumade* (a common rake) and *masakari* (ax).

One semi-formalized combat system was known as *timbei,* and its practitioners used a small shield of leather stretched on a wooden frame. The shield was called a *to-hai,* and it had a peephole cut in it for the fighter to look through. Parrying with the *to-hai,* the fighter would counterattack with a *hera,* an implement normally used for harvesting rice.

Again, the primary contribution of the Okinawans to weaponry was not their invention of these weapons, for virtually all of the tools they used were in common usage throughout Southeast Asia. Indeed, the primary contribution of the Okinawans lay in their ingenious application of their tools to warfare.

In unarmed combat, too, the Okinawans displayed an ingenuity virtually unsurpassed in its clever use of body dynamics.

Until the 19th century, the Okinawans referred to their empty-handed combat arts as *te,* which means, simply, "hands." As trade developed with other countries, the foreigners took notice of Okinawan boxing and called it *Okinawa-te,* to distinguish it from other forms of fighting found in the South Seas.

Even though the art developed in semi-secrecy, its individual exponents became highly renowned in Okinawa, and many young men sought to train under the guidance of the various masters. More often than not, they sought out a teacher of *tode,* the name by which the art had come to be known among most Okinawans in the mid-1800s. I is an alternative rendering and pronunciation of *kara,* which means "Chinese" and refers specifically to things of Chinese origin in the *T'ang* Dynasty.

By the turn of the century, judo and kendo had been introduced to Okinawa from Japan, and they enjoyed great curiosity, if not widespread popularity. Nevertheless, the Okinawans were quick to adopt formal Japanese terminology in describing their own, indigenous fighting arts, and by the time karate was openly taught to the public in 1905, it was generally known as karate-jutsu. *Kara* was reflective of Chinese influences on the art, *te* indicated its Okinawan origins, and *jutsu* was a polite employment of Japanese terminology. In this way, the Okinawans paid homage to the Japanese, the Chinese, and their own masters.

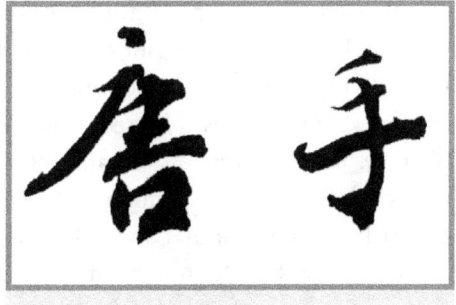

TO DE

By the time of the Meiji Restoration (1868), *tode* experts were developing highly individualistic styles of the art, and some of them were famous figures in the local folklore. By the turn of the century, when karate was first openly taught and incorporated into the public school system, many different "styles" of the art had been more or less formalized. Each style bore the distinctions of its originators and masters, and each had developed distinctive *kata* (formal exercises) for use in teaching the art to students.

Literally hundreds of different styles of karate were extant on Okinawa in the early 1900s, but few of them were styles in the sense in which "style" is used today. Indeed, an entire "style" might consist of only one farmer whose specialty was punching, or one fisherman whose specialty was kicking. Most of the turn of the century karate masters on Okinawa were noted for only one or two techniques. One master, for instance, is purported to have practiced only the reverse elbow strike, day after day, year after year, until the end of his long life. It was not until the early 1900s that complete systems incorporating varied methods of blocking, punching, kicking, and striking appeared.

When Gichin Funakoshi took karate to Japan in 1922, he wrote in his first book a description of the general characteristics of what he perceived to be the different styles of Okinawan karate, and it was his descriptions that, more than anything else, encouraged the masters on Okinawa to begin classifying their own arts in terms of style.

The two most prominent styles of karate on Okinawa were the Kobayashi Shorin-ryu, which was characterized by high, light movements of the body, reminiscent of the techniques of northern Chinese boxing, and the Shoreiji-ryu, which was characterized by low, solid stances and the heavy muscular techniques of southern Chinese boxing. As will be seen later, when Funakoshi described his new, Japanese version of karate-jutsu, he described the kata in terms of "Shorin" and "Shorei."

Still another popular style of karate on Okinawa was the "hard-soft" style, which formed the basis of Gogen Yamaguchi's famous Japanese Goju style. It was introduced in Naha by Kanryo Higaonna (1852–1915), after 20 years of training in China under Liu Liu Ko, a famous Chinese boxer. In the 1890s, he introduced the *kata,* Sanchin, which, with its slow and deep respirations, represents the essence of the hard-soft qualities of Goju-ryu. Following in Higaonna's footsteps was Chojun Miyagi (1888–1953), who formally named the system Goju-ryu.

Once karate was permitted to be practiced in the open, its masters moved quickly to improve it, expand the number of people studying it, and to formalize various training methods and practice routines. Also, once these masters had more opportunity to observe each other in action, they borrowed ideas and techniques freely from one another. By 1915, for example, almost all the schools of karate were using similar training equipment.

Since the development of karate on Okinawa had always been centered on hardening the body and making it impervious to blows, the Okinawans devised many pieces of equipment to further the body-hardening process.

First and foremost among these training devices, and the only one which is universally used today in virtually all styles of karate-do, was the *makiwara*. Literally, *makiwara* means "straw wrapped rope," and that is exactly what it consisted of in its original form. The main structure of the makiwara consisted of a long board, about three feet of it implanted in the ground, and about four or five feet of it protruding above ground. A sheaf of straw tied with hemp was tied securely to the board, and the trainee would spend hours every day punching and striking the straw pad. Today, the straw is usually replaced by heavy, shock-absorbent rubber, but the resultant strengthening of the body parts used in executing powerful punches and strikes remains the same.

Makiwara

Another device, which is still popular today, was *tetsugeta,* or "iron clogs."

These heavy *geta* were worn on the feet during hundreds or even thousands of slow repetitions of kicks and stepping patterns. Precursors of modern ankle weights, the *geta* provided an extra strengthening effect by

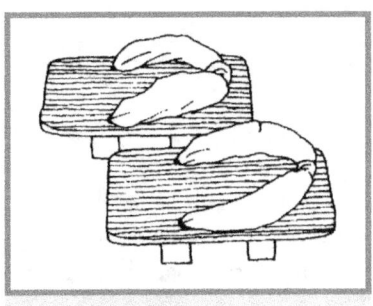

Iron Geta

The Okinawan Roots

requiring the user to firmly grip the leather thongs with his toes. Losing the toe grip on the thongs could send a heavy *geta* flying—a dangerous situation for both the user and his fellow trainees.

Kame

First cousins of the *tetsugeta* were the *sashi,* or handheld weights. These did for the arms what the *tetsugeta* purported to do for the feet and legs, and their use was widespread. Other uniquely Okinawan training devices, which are no longer in general use in most Japanese karate dojo, included *kame,* heavy clay or earthenware jars, sometimes filled with sand or water, which were gripped and held or carried for long periods of time to strengthen the grip.

Other muscle-strengthening devices included the *chikaraishi* (power stone) and *makiage-gu* (a rack with a bar and weight).

The power stone was held by a handle attached to a heavy stone, and the practitioner would swing the stone in various patterns of techniques, and sometimes would twirl the stone by the handle, and then grasp it tightly at the impact point of a punch, strike, or block.

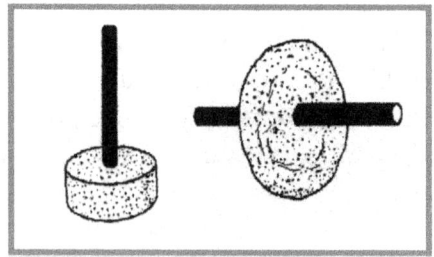
Chikaraishi (Power Stone)

The *makiage-gu,* on the other hand, was an early Okinawan version of modern weight training equipment. A heavy stone was tied to a rope, which in turn was tied securely to a bar about four feet off the ground.

The students would place one or both hands on the bar, and

would roll the bar, first in one direction and then the other, raising the stone and lowering it. The purpose of this practice was to develop strong wrists and forearms, and as the practitioner's strength increased, heavier stones could be attached to the rope.

Other popular devices and methods, designed more for the purpose of hardening specific parts of the body than for general strengthening, were the *kakete-biki* (a lever bar) and the method known as *kanshu* (penetration hand).

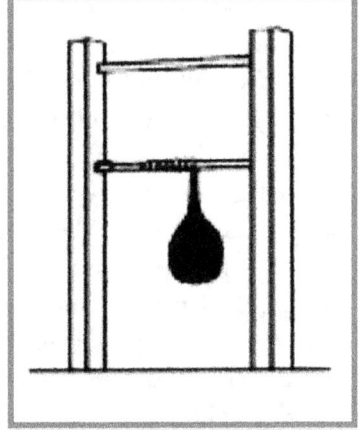

Makiage-gu

Kakete-biki

The *kakete-biki* was a rather complicated lever bar that could be struck with various techniques of the hands and arms, and then grasped, pulled, and kicked.

It was a rather severe training device for the connective tissues of the body, and it resembled the modern wing chun wooden dummy, which enjoys popularity among some Chinese martial artists today.

Kanshu, or "penetration hand," also was not the most healthful of pursuits among Okinawan martial artists, but for the purpose of making the fingers and hands impervious to pain, it was surpassed in effectiveness only by the makiwara. In *kanshu* training, the trainee would stand astride a bucket or deep pan filled with fine powder. He would thrust his stiffened fingers into the powder again and again, until, after a long period of training, he could thrust all the way to the bottom of the container without difficulty. As soon as this was accomplished, rice, a harder substance, would be substituted for the powder, and the process repeated. As the trainee's hands became more impervious to pain, harder materials would be used, graduating from powder and rice to sand, dried beans and, finally, small pebbles. As might be guessed, the hands of longtime practitioners of *kanshu* often would be grotesque in appearance, but, as might also be guessed, those hands often could pierce several inches of pine or fir with a single thrust of rigid fingertips.

When Gichin Funakoshi transported karate-jutsu from Okinawa to Japan, he took along the primary training devices of *makiwara, tetsugeta,* and *sashi,* and while later Okinawan masters introduced other Okinawan training devices to Japan proper, most of these devices were rarely used on a regular basis by the Japanese.

The most important contribution of the Okinawans in general to modern karate-do was their development of the individual techniques of punching, striking, kicking, and blocking, and their development and transmission of *kata,* the formal exercises containing the essential techniques and movements of their individual styles.

The actual transformation of the diverse techniques and methods of Okinawan karate-jutsu into the coherent, organized system known today as karate-do, is largely the work of a single man: the Okinawan karate-jutsu master, Gichin Funakoshi.

2
Gichin Funakoshi
The Man and the Myth

Some five million people in 65 countries around the world regularly leave their homes, travel to an unimposing building, put on a white cotton uniform, and submit themselves to some of the strictest physical discipline found outside of prisons. They do this voluntarily. Indeed, when they have no money, they frequently ask for more discipline in the form of washing windows, scrubbing floors and toilets, and generally sweeping up in exchange for the right to continue receiving this particular form of individual torture.

Their disease is not limited to any special stratum of society: these strange people are male and female, young and old, black and white, red and yellow, ill and well, tall, thin, short, stout, and they span all generations. They are not a religious or fanatical cult, and getting any two of them to agree on anything more serious than lunch is decidedly impossible. While they do not collectively agree on much of anything, there is one thing on which they always agree: Shotokan karate-do is a wonderful way of life.

Virtually without exception, serious students of Shotokan karate-do represent the antithesis of the widely held public image of "karate people." They wear only white uniforms, and can rarely, if ever, be found wearing a bellbottomed, lace-up, elasticized waist, custom-trimmed gi. The few who wear patches on their gi disdain dragons and snakes, and their belts (even black belts) are never marked with stripes or stars.

Acknowledging that there may be exceptions to every rule, it can still be said with a high degree of certitude that serious students of Shotokan karate-do are a different breed. They simply do not fit the modern mold. What they do fit is their plain cotton gi, and it is in those gi that, hour after hour, day after day, year after year, they strive mightily toward a narrow ideal conceived by an indigent school teacher more than 70 years ago. Their teachers tell them to "move from center," "find your spirit," and divine the meaning of *ikken hisatsu* ("to kill with one blow"). They are not unfamiliar with jumping and spinning and slashing, but *ikken hisatsu* is difficult to find when one is flying through the air; it is more likely to be found rooted in the earth.

A common bond shared by Shotokan people (and guarded zealously by them) is the knowledge that their karate derives from the direct lineage of the first master who introduced karate to the Japanese people. There is a "correctness" to it, which is supported by the tree of tradition. There are new branches sprouting out now and then, but it will take them at least 50 more years to prove themselves worthy of the trunk. The master, you see, left Shotokan people not only with a firmly rooted tree of tradition, but also with the charge to grow, multiply, expand, and become stronger. *"Shu-ha-ri"* he called it: "Learn from tradition, break the bonds of tradition, transcend tradition, and find something new. At the end, you will find what you started with: tradition."

No matter how new or how good or how unique a style or innovation may be, it must face the same problem (which is the problem the master gave them in the beginning and left them with in the end): how do you make a stronger punch, a stronger kick, a better person? It is to this riddle that Shotokan people assiduously apply themselves. And with the strength of punch and kick of the current Shotokan masters, it is a riddle that most of the students never get around to solving—at least not by innovation. Indeed, they are proud of their legacy and the mysteries it nurtures. And a rich legacy it is, too.

Gichin Funakoshi, "the father of modern karate-do" (as Shotokan people prefer to call him), was born to a privileged class *(shizoku)* in Shuri, Okinawa, in 1868. His birth coincided with the Meiji Reformation of 1868, in which official class privilege was abolished. The *kuge* (court nobles) and *daimyo* (provincial lords) were assigned the title of *kizoku* or "peers," and the samurai were relegated to the position of *shizoku* or "gentry."

Funakoshi's father, Gisu Tominakoshi (Tominakoshi being the original rendering of the family name), was a lower-ranking official of the privileged class, whose only son, Gichin, was born prematurely-a condition that in those days was a harbinger of ill health and a short life. As was the custom, the frail child was given over to his maternal grandmother for rearing and the extra care that only she would know how to give. Regardless of health or special care, it was essential for sons of the *shizoku* to be schooled carefully in the Chinese Classics, and Funakoshi's grandfather began this tutelage as soon as Gichin was old enough to talk.

One popular myth is that Funakoshi's father took Gichin to Yasutsune Azato, the great scholar and karate master, and implored Azato to teach the boy karate to improve his health. In fact, Funakoshi's father, an alcoholic who squandered the family fortune on drink, had nothing at all to do with Gichin's introduction to karate. While attending primary school, Gichin became enamored of a playmate who could perform fancy tricks with his body. The playmate was the son of Azato, and the two boys, at the age of 11, simply started "playing at" karate under the watchful eyes of Azato.

As Funakoshi's health began to improve, his doctor, Tokashiki, urged Funakoshi's grandfather to approach Azato with a formal request to accept the young Gichin as a student. Azato did accept Funakoshi, and the course of the boy's life was changed completely.

In later life, Funakoshi credited his health and longevity to the care of Tokashiki and the physical and mental discipline he received from Azato.

As young Funakoshi grew toward manhood, his interest in karate grew stronger. Night after night, he would walk in the dark, sometimes carrying a dim lantern, to Azato's house and would there place himself in the *sensei's* (teacher's) hands. While the physical discipline was rigorous, it shared equal status with the learning of more Chinese classics and the study of Confucian dialectics. Azato himself was a scholar of the Wan Yang Ming (or "Mind") school of Confucianism, which taught that the mental and physical aspects of man must not be separated, and he therefore challenged his pupils with both physical and intellectual exercises. He instilled in them the importance of *igen,* the unaffected, permeating dignity of demeanor required of sons of *shizoku.*

Primarily because of Azato's tutelage, Funakoshi was able to pass the tests for becoming a school teacher in 1888. His teaching career in the primary, middle, and upper schools was to last for more than 30 years.

Because of his attachment to Azato, Funakoshi was able to meet and train under many of the best karate masters of the day in Okinawa, most notably Itosu, Kiyuna, Niigaki, Toono, and the great "Bushi" Matsumura.

Another popular myth is that Funakoshi was poor because he

spent all his time practicing karate and not enough time working for the direct benefit of his family. One would be hard pressed to find a myth more completely absurd.

Funakoshi's life on Okinawa was indeed poverty-stricken, but the circumstances of his penurious existence had nothing to do with karate. For many years, Funakoshi's family had been attached to a lower-ranking clan of officials, and his paternal grandfather, Gifuku, had been generously rewarded for his years of faithful service with a house at Tairamachi on a highly valued piece of ground near the Kuntoku Daikun Goten shrine. This, along with a substantial sum of money, was given to Funakoshi's father as his legacy. Funakoshi's father, however, was an alcoholic who quickly dissipated the family's wealth and his own health with liquor. Since Gichin was the only son, he bore the responsibility for the care and feeding of his family—his wife, their children, both sets of parents, and all the living grandparents. At the age of 21, Funakoshi embarked on a career as a school teacher to support this exceedingly large family, and as a school teacher, he was forbidden by the Department of Education to hold another job. He and his wife, therefore, grew virtually all of the food the family had to eat, and Funakoshi frequently disguised himself in a peasant's outfit (it was unbecoming for a school teacher to tend the fields) and worked in a small communal field with his wife, planting, tending, and harvesting the rice and vegetables.

Through all of this, Funakoshi continued his karate training, not for profit, but because he by now sincerely believed that karate was what had given him his health and maintained both the physical and mental strength required for his arduous life.

Through all of Funakoshi's training, karate was practiced only underground. The Okinawans, having had their weapons banned over the course of about 400 years, were forced to practice unarmed self-defense in secrecy. This, of course, is why Funakoshi had to practice and train at night, surreptitiously sneaking down the roads with a dimly lit lantern, finding his way to the house of Azato. Not until Funakoshi was past 30 years old was karate considered benign enough to be demonstrated and practiced in the open.

It is believed that Yasutsune Itosu's instruction of karate to selected gym classes at the Shurijijo Elementary School was the first time the art was taught in a group class setting. Itosu was Funakoshi's other, primary instructor, along with Yasutsune Azato.

The first formal, recorded demonstration of the art was performed by Funakoshi in 1902 for Shintaro Ogawa, Commissioner of Schools for Kagoshima Prefecture. Funakoshi was by this time teaching his own young charges, and he used these young men to demonstrate the value of karate as physical and mental conditioning. So taken was Ogawa with the sincerity of the man and the vigor of the youths, that he recommended to the Ministry of Education that Funakoshi's karate be instituted on a formal basis in the Okinawan school system.

To the surprise of many other masters of the art, some of whom had come to cherish the idea of keeping the art secret, karate was quickly approved as a physical education program at both the Men's Normal School in Shuri and at the Prefectural Daiichi Middle School. Because of Funakoshi's academic and philosophical approach to karate, the art quickly attracted the interest of the intellectuals and educators of the day, and Funakoshi, an educator himself, was always available to demonstrate and explain.

Yasutsune Itosu oversaw the development of karate in the middle schools, and in 1905 made the first recorded attempt to provide karate with a competitive, sporting aspect. Hardly a sport by modern standards, the karate introduced to the schools by Itosu and Funakoshi nevertheless afforded the young students an opportunity to test their skills against one another within the traditional framework of *hitotsuki, hitogeri* ("one punch, one kick").

By 1905, karate clubs had been established at the Okinawaken Middle School, the Prefectural Agricultural School, the Prefectural Fisheries College, the Naha City School of Commerce, and others. In most cases, the "competition" consisted mainly of groups of students from the various schools getting together and performing a *kata* in front of the rest of the group, with the group then commenting about the skillfulness of the performance.

Throughout his life on Okinawa, Funakoshi was first a school teacher and secondarily a karate teacher. By gaining the approval of the Ministry of Education to teach karate in the schools, he was able to blend vocation with avocation, and his reputation spread in both academic and karate circles.

Shortly after conducting the first organized public exhibition of karate in 1906, Funakoshi was offered various promotions in the school system, some of which he accepted, and some of which he refused because they would take him too far away from the source of his karate training.

By 1913, requests for public and private demonstrations of karate had grown to such proportions that Funakoshi formally organized a demonstration "team" composed of the most active karate masters of the day. This group, which included the great masters Choki Motobu (the most colorful and controversial figure in the history of Okinawan karate), Chotoku Kyan (the master most responsible for the development of the myriad styles of Shorin-ryu karate), Moden Yahiku (a well-known student of Itosu), Kenwa Mabuni (later the founder of the enormously popular Shito-ryu style of karate), and about 20 lesser-known experts of the time, toured Okinawa constantly during the period 1914-1915, and gave countless demonstrations of the art to thousands of people. More often than not, Funakoshi would narrate while the others demonstrated, always taking care to explain the importance of karate as a method of developing character and self-discipline. When he demonstrated personally, he usually performed the *kata,* Koshokun (now commonly called Kanku Dai), and told the crowds that this *kata* contained all the essential elements of karate.

While the Japanese characteristically showed very little, if any, interest in indigenous Okinawan arts, they were more than passingly interested in karate. Many of them saw Funakoshi and his troupe demonstrating, and carried stories back with them to the

Japanese mainland. They told wondrous tales of seeing men jumping up from a standing position and kicking the ceiling; of seeing slightly built Okinawans smashing a thick stack of roofing tiles with a single blow; and of the almost timid little school teacher who seemed to be in charge of it all.

Since karate was by this time deeply entrenched in the Okinawan schools, it was not surprising that the Ministry of Education asked Funakoshi to demonstrate his art in Japan. So, in 1917, the poor schoolteacher traveled to Kyoto and demonstrated karate for the first time in Japan at the Butokuden. While the demonstration was successful and Japanese interest was high, there was no immediate rush to bring the Okinawan art to Japan on a formal basis. As taken as they were with it, the Japanese still tended to be suspicious of anything purely Okinawan, and they found it expedient to view karate as an interesting sideshow.

With the exception of Funakoshi's demonstration in Japan, the only recorded demonstration outside of Okinawa during this period was conducted by Kentsu Yabu, a truly outstanding student of Matsumura and a junior to Yasutsune Itosu. In February 1920, Yabu demonstrated karate in Hawaii, and in fact taught the rudiments of the art to a small group of Okinawans and Japanese who had emigrated to Los Angeles.

Even though karate was gaining more notoriety, even internationally, the Japanese were still reluctant to embrace it. This attitude could have been the end of karate in Japan had it not been for a fortuitous event on March 6, 1921. On that date, the Crown Prince (who later became the Emperor Hirohito) of Japan visited Okinawa on his way to Europe. Seeking to show the Prince the unique development of Okinawan youth and to impress him with the rich cultural heritage of Okinawa, the Department of Education asked Funakoshi to give a karate demonstration for him in the Great Hall of Shuri Castle. So fascinated was the Prince by the demonstration, that he spoke of it excitedly throughout the rest of his voyage.

With such positive official approval of an Okinawan art, word

Gichin Funakoshi

Gichin Funakoshi (Center row, seated 2nd from left) and his students on the occasion of their demonstration of karate for the Crown Prince at Shuri Castle on March 6, 1921

soon filtered down from above that the Prince would like to see karate again. Thus it was that the Ministry of Education issued a formal request for a karate demonstration to be performed at the first National Athletic Exhibition in Tokyo.

Since it was well known that Funakoshi's demonstration had pleased the Crown Prince, and since Funakoshi was President of the Okinawan Shobukai (Okinawan Martial Spirit Promotion Society), he was the most logical choice to carry karate to the Japanese people in an official capacity.

Many Shotokan people today take pride in their assertion that Gichin Funakoshi was the most proficient of all karate men on Okinawa, and was chosen for that reason. This prideful assertion is common, but has little basis in fact. Clearly, Funakoshi was not the most experienced karate man on Okinawa; several highly proficient people were senior to Funakoshi. While it is beyond question that Funakoshi was extraordinarily proficient, it also is clear that he probably would have been chosen to demonstrate karate to the Japanese people regardless of the level of his physical prowess.

What was unique about Funakoshi in Okinawa was that he was the most highly educated, scholarly, and articulate man in karate. He was well acquainted with Japanese customs and manners, and he was completely fluent in the Japanese language—traits not shared by other Okinawan karate masters. Funakoshi also displayed a unique trait not displayed by the others: he was openly and fervently dedicated to the promotion and propagation of karate as a method of self-discipline, health, and character development.

It was Funakoshi, in fact, who founded the Okinawan Shobukai, and it was he who, more than any of his peers, insisted on raising the goals of karate to that of a humanistic art.

With his characteristic devotion and energy, Funakoshi threw himself—body, mind, and spirit—into preparation for the trip to Japan. In his beautiful calligraphy, he wrote three large scrolls describing the history and basic techniques of karate, and embellished the scrolls with photographs of karate techniques.

While on the ship to Japan, Funakoshi felt, for the first time perhaps, the gigantic proportions of the significance of his journey, and he set down his thoughts in a poem:

> On the island in the sea to the south,
> There is transmitted an exquisite art.
> This is karate.
> To my great regret,
> The art has declined
> and its transmission is in doubt.
> Who would undertake
> The monumental task
> of restoration and revival?
> This task I must undertake;
> Who would if I did not?
> I vowed to the blue sky.[1]

Gichin Funakoshi

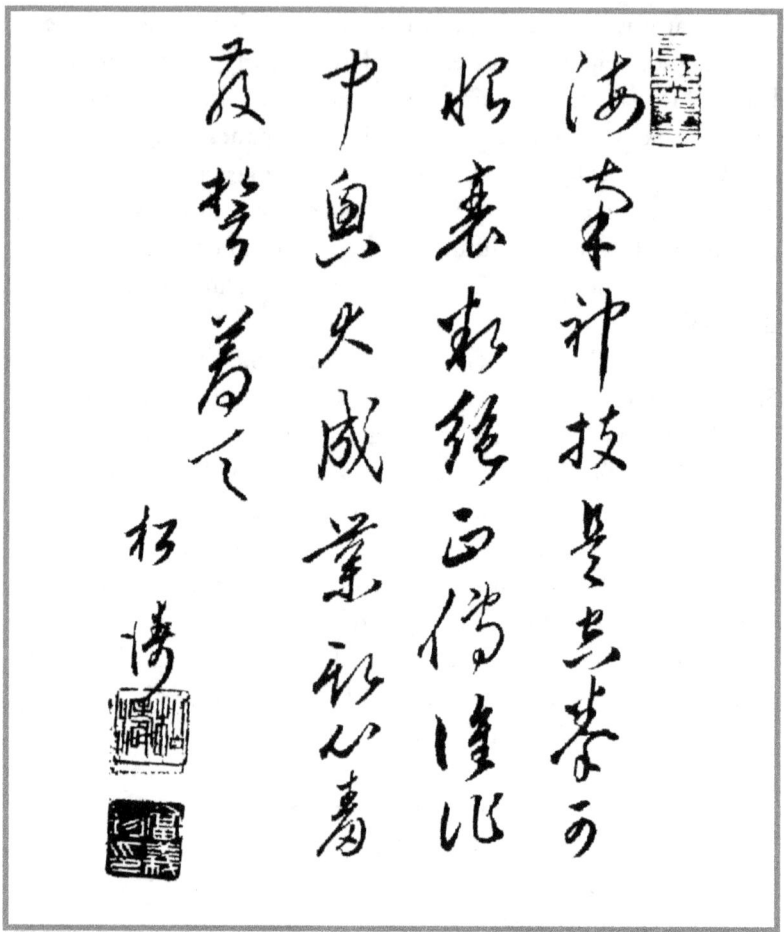

Ji Fun Shi "A Full Determination" Poem in Gichin Funakoshi's own calligraphy, penned while he was traveling from Okinawa to Japan in 1922

With these thoughts in mind and scrolls in hand, Gichin Funakoshi formally introduced karate to the Japanese people at the Women's Higher Normal School in Tokyo on April 1, 1922.

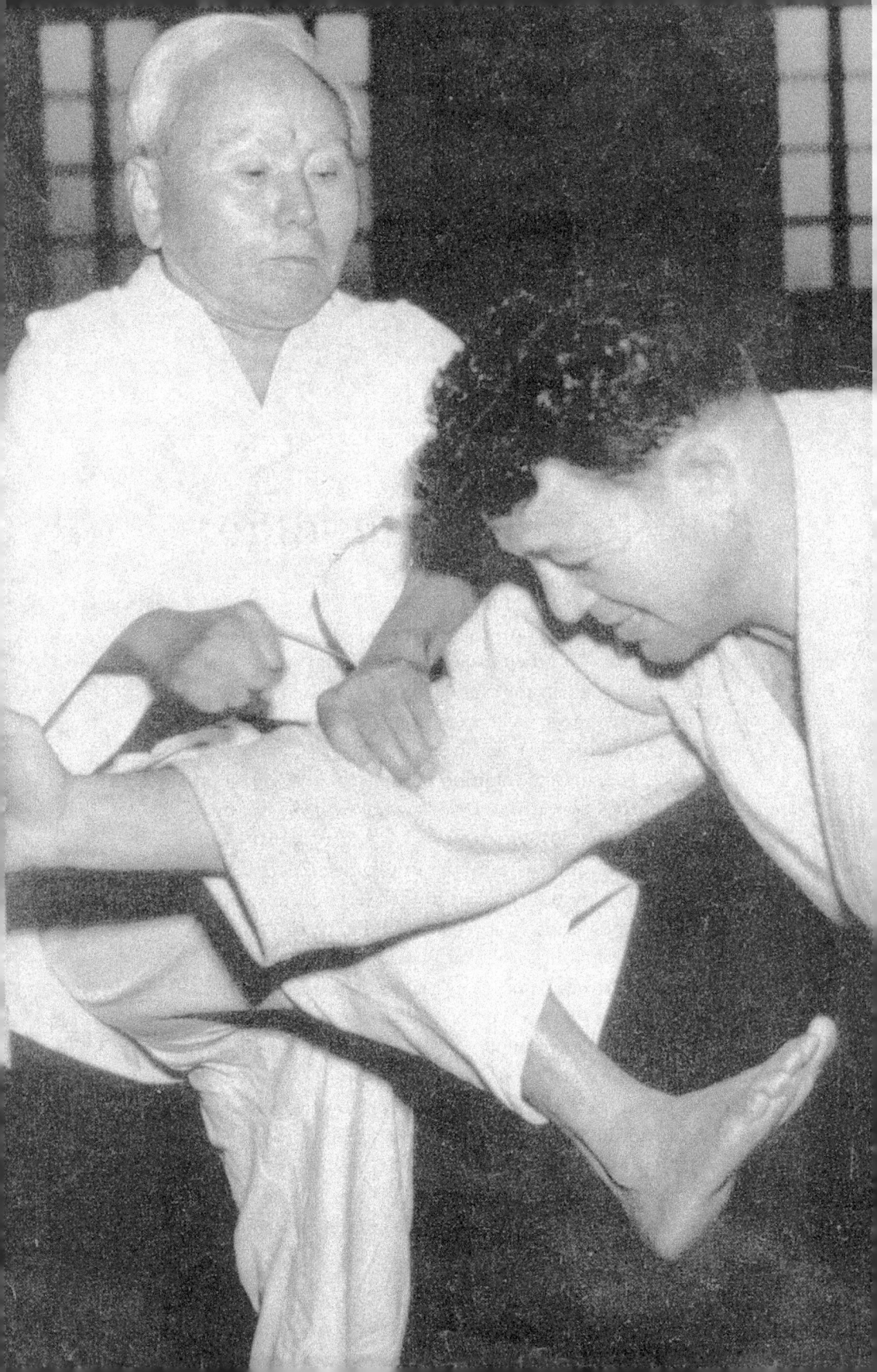

3
Karate Comes to Japan

The first National Athletic Exhibition was a very important event for the Japanese. With their growing nationalism and militarism, they took great pride in the athletic prowess of their people, and representatives from virtually every upper level of society attended to applaud the young men and women.

By 1922, the martial tradition occupied a large segment of Japanese athletics. As early as 1895, the government had established the Dai Nippon Butokukai (Great Japan Martial Virtues Association) in Kyoto. In 1899, the Butokuden (Martial Virtues Hall) was built in Kyoto adjacent to the Heian Shrine, and a select group of the finest budo masters were paid to teach there. In 1911, the Dai Nippon Butokukai Bujutsu Semmon Gakko (Great Japan Martial Virtues Association Martial Arts Specialty School) was established at the Butokuden, and masters of various *ryu* from all over Japan regularly taught and lectured there. Also in 1911, the Ministry of Education made it mandatory for middle school students to select either judo or kendo as a required subject. Thus, by the time of the first National Athletic Exhibition, virtually all members of the upper classes were duty bound to attend and applaud the skills of the young people.

The attendance of so many prominent and influential people

Shotokan Karate: Its History and Evolution

turned out to be the key factor in the direction and scope of Gichin Funakoshi's life from that moment until his death.

Jigoro Kano

To say that the Japanese were strongly attracted to Funakoshi and his karate is a gross understatement. On the same day he gave the demonstration, he was approached by members of the Sho family, direct descendants of Shotai, the last King of Okinawa, and was asked to extend his visit to Japan to give more demonstrations. Humbled and inspired by their supplications, Funakoshi agreed to stay for a few weeks. And it was in those "few weeks" that the course of karate was forever altered. First came a request from Jigoro Kano, the famous and brilliant founder of judo, to demonstrate karate at the Kodokan, the judo headquarters. To assist him with the demonstration, Funakoshi prevailed upon Shinkin Gima, a student at Tokyo Shoka Daigaku, who had attained a high degree of proficiency in karate while still in Okinawa. At a private demonstration for Kano and selected members of the Kodokan, Funakoshi performed the *kata,* Kanku Dai, and Gima performed Naihanchi (which is now known to the Japanese as Tekki). So impressed was Kano by the demonstration and the intelligence and sincerity of the little man, that he enthusiastically implored Funakoshi to stay in Japan a bit longer to teach him the basics of karate. Funakoshi did indeed teach Kano some of the most basic blocks, punches, strikes, and kicks, and Kano later incorporated some of these into an advanced judo kata.

Sensing Funakoshi's overabundant humility, Kano graciously treated him as a peer and introduced him to many influential Japanese, always extolling the virtues of Funakoshi as a master of a

Karate Comes to Japan

wonderful and important martial art. Kano well knew that Funakoshi possessed both the physical and intellectual capacity to make karate grow and flourish in Japan, and he did everything he could to encourage Funakoshi to pursue such goals. Kano acted as Funakoshi's psychological mentor, counseling him when he was depressed, and bolstering his spirits when he was homesick.

In later years, after Kano's passing, Funakoshi would always stop as he passed the Kodokan and offer a silent prayer or, if he was riding by on a streetcar, he would tip his hat. Many of his students who accompanied him on his trips were perplexed by this, and often asked him why he was always praying for judo. "I'm not praying for judo," Funakoshi always told them. "I'm offering a prayer and respect to the spirit of Jigoro Kano. Without him, I would not be here today."

The demonstration at the National Athletic Exhibition, along with Kano's introductions, soon led to official requests for karate instruction from the military academy, the Tokyo Bar Association, and the Society for Research in High School Physical Education. While eager to demonstrate and teach for these groups, Funakoshi was still grappling with homesickness, worry about his family, and guilt over leaving his responsibilities behind.

Finally, the famous painter, Hoan Kosugi, President of the Tabata Poplar Club, an artist's guild, asked Funakoshi to teach karate to the members of the club. Following a lesson one day, he implored Funakoshi to consider how important karate training was for all the people he was teaching, and to carefully consider whether he could, in good conscience, deny all these people the benefits of his instruction. After correspondence with his wife, in which she gave her blessing, Gichin Funakoshi irrevocably decided to stay in Japan and fulfill what he now perceived as his God-given destiny: He would teach karate to the Japanese people. His whole life up to this point, he believed, had been a preparation for this great mission.

While the Japanese in general were reluctant to embrace anything of Okinawan extraction, they were more than eager to pursue almost anything pursued by the upper classes. While karate did not sweep the general populace like a gale, it flourished like a hula hoop craze among the upper classes.

In June 1922, the *Tokyo Nichinichi* introduced karate to the Japanese public with the headline, "Karate—The Mysterious Martial Art Wrath Produced." This article, the first ever published in Japan on the subject of karate, emphasized the terrifying and sensational aspects of the art. Funakoshi's karate, the article emphasized, was an insidious art that could kill a man by crushing his internal organs without damaging his skin or muscles. However, the article also quoted Funakoshi as saying, "Essentially, the principal purpose of karate is defense. The initial move has long been strictly prohibited, and it is said that there is no initial move in karate *(karate ni sente nashi)*. This martial art is to cultivate a modest mind, which must not become uselessly carried away by the martial spirit. Moreover, it requires no weapon. So I think it is most suitable as a civilized self-defense art. Furthermore, it is effective for the training of one's body, since the limbs are moved in a well-coordinated manner. In my observation, there is no doubt that it helps you to live long."

In less than nine months, karate had become "the" fad for the intelligentsia, and Funakoshi proved himself worthy of the challenge. In 1922 he established the first formal Japanese karate club at the Meisei Juku, a dormitory and school for newly arrived Okinawan students in the Suidobata section of Tokyo. To support himself, he cleaned the dormitory during the day, often tending the garden and lawns, and taught karate in a lecture hall in the evening. Throwing himself completely into his mission, he wrote the first book on karate titled, *Ryukyu Kempo: Karate*. Published by Bukyosha in 1922, the book contained separate forewords written by such luminaries as Prince Hisamasa, the former governor of Okinawa; Admiral Rokuro Yashiro; Vice Admiral Chosei Ogasawara; Prince Shimpei Goto; Rear Admiral Norikazu Kanna; Professor Norihiro Tono; and journalist Bakumonto Sueyoshi of the *Okinawa Times*. The writing venture was undertaken largely at the prodding of Hoan Kosugi, a famous artist, who agreed to design the book if Funakoshi would write it.

An instant bestseller by textbook standards, the book contained chapters titled "What Karate Is," "The Value of Karate," "Karate Training and Teaching," "The Organization of Karate," "Fundamentals and Kata," and an appendix containing "Precautions on Practice."

The primary *kata* introduced in this book included Heian Shodan, Heian Nidan, Heian Sandan, Heian Yondan, Heian Godan, Naihanchi Shodan, Naihanchi Nidan, Naihanchi Sandan, Bassai Dai, Bassai Sho, Kanku Dai, Kanku Sho, Jion, Jutte, Chinte, Gojushiho, Chinto, Seishan, Sochin, Rohai, Wankuan, Unsu, Ji'in, Kokan, Wanshu, Wandau, Jumu, Wando, Niseshi, Suparinpei and Sanseryu.

In the introduction Funakoshi inscribed his ideals of karate for the Japanese People. In it, he spoke of the "seeds of destruction" that "lurk deep within the shadows of human nature." He lamented the decline of physical fitness of young men in Japan, and suggested that karate was an art that would raise the level of health, strength, and vitality of the nation's youth. He warned against complacency and said that the "sword and the pen are as inseparable as the two wheels of a cart… A man must encompass both fields if he is to be considered a man of accomplishment"[1]

The initial success of this book was stunted, for a time, when the plates for the book were destroyed in the Great Kanto Earthquake on September 1, 1923. Following the devastation of the earthquake, the book was not printed again until 1926, at which time it was reissued by Kobundo as *Rentan Goshin Karate-jutsu* ("Strengthening of Willpower and Self-defense Through Techniques of Karate.")

Many of Funakoshi's finest young pupils were lost in the earthquake also, and he was forced to take a job making stencils at the Daiichi Sogo Bank at Kyobashi. Since this was quite some distance from the Meisei Juku, Funakoshi was invited to move his dojo to the kendo dojo of Hakudo Nakayama, the great kendo teacher and founder of modern iaido.

The significance of Nakayama's offer cannot be overestimated, for in Japanese thinking, the dojo is "the place where the way is studied," and it is a sacred place, not to be treated lightly nor used for any other purpose. For a great kendo sensei to hold another art in such high esteem that he would allow it to be practiced in his dojo was unprecedented. Thus, even with the devastation of the earthquake, Funakoshi (through the graciousness of Hakudo Nakayama) managed to keep the interest in karate alive.

At the age of 56, when most men are contemplating retirement, he entered and qualified in the Tokyo Invitational Prize Contest for Athletes, and was therefore granted permission to give a formal karate demonstration at the Jichi Hall ("Hall of Self-Government") at Ueno, Tokyo, in 1924. With the attendant publicity surrounding this event, karate was once again on its way to popularity.

Throughout the 1920s and early 1930s, Funakoshi continued to teach at Nakayama's kendo dojo, and the number of active students increased steadily, until his fame garnered him an invitation to demonstrate karate for the Imperial Household in the Sainei-Kan hall on the palace grounds. In later years, Funakoshi fondly recalled this demonstration, on March 20, 1928, as one of the brightest points in his entire life. It was just incredible and unthinkable (to Funakoshi perhaps more than others) that a "foreigner" would receive a personal invitation from the Imperial Household Agency to actually set foot on the palace grounds—much less demonstrate for the royal family. But word of Funakoshi's demonstration with 15 of his students spread quickly, and karate was once again given a significant boost from the royal family.

Between 1920 and 1928, karate was growing steadily, primarily through the universities and colleges, but also through instruction to groups of employees at companies such as the Tokyo Department Store and Railroad Company, the Matsuzakaya Department Stores, and others.

Karate Comes to Japan

In 1924, Funakoshi was asked by Professor Shinyo Kasuya of the Department of German Language and Literature at Keio University to teach a group of students at the university. Funakoshi was quick to accept the invitation, and the club was soon organized on a formal basis with the sanction of the university. The Keio club was the first collegiate karate club in Japan, and it is active to this day.

In 1925, students from various other colleges started coming to Funakoshi for instruction, and they gradually organized clubs on their campuses over the course of the next few years. In 1926 the Tokyo University Karate Club was officially chartered, and was followed in the early 1930s by clubs at Takushoku, Chuo, Shodai (now called Hitotsubashi University), Gakushuin, Hosei, Nihon, Meiji, and others, until today there are over 200 collegiate karate clubs in Japan.

Not only did the popularization of karate at the university level help spread the art in Japan, but later exerted a highly significant influence on the internationalization of Shotokan karate in the 1960s.

The growth of Funakoshi's karate continued unabated throughout the 1930s, and its popularity spawned several other *ryu* (schools or styles). In 1928, Nippon Kempo was introduced by Muneomi Sawayama, and was organized into the All Japan Kempo Federation in 1935. Also in 1928, Kenwa Mabuni, an Okinawan contemporary of Funakoshi who also studied with Yasutsune Itosu, introduced a style called Shito-ryu in Osaka after a period of study with the great master of Nahate, Kanryo Higaonna.

Kanryo Higaonna

Kenwa Mabuni, Founder of Shito Ryu Karate

Gogen "The Cat" Yamaguchi

In a poor choice of words, Mabuni originally called his style "Hanko," which was often translated as "Half-heart." The name Shito was derived by Mabuni from alternate pronunciations of the characters used to write the names of his instructors ("Shi" is from the "Ito" of Itosu, and "to" is from the "Higa" of Higaonna).

Gogen Yamaguchi, a disciple of Chojun Miyagi, introduced the Goju-ryu ("Hard-Soft") style of karate in Tokyo in 1930, defining it as *seishin no mono,* "a thing of the spirit."

Statue of Chojun Miyagi, founder of Goju-ryu karate

Karate Comes to Japan

Hironori Ohtsuka (right), in 1968, performs his famous demonstration against sword attack against his son (also named Hironori).

Teruo Hayashi

In 1931 Kanken Toyama introduced a style called Shudokan, and in 1933, with the founding of the Dai Nippon Butokukai, Okinawa Branch, karate was listed as an official Japanese martial art.

Also notable among the early pioneers of karate in Japan was Hironori Ohtsuka, who introduced the Wado-ryu ("Way of Peace") style in 1939. Ohtsuka, one of the most senior disciples of Funakoshi, was also the inheritor of the leadership of two separate styles of jujutsu, and these he combined to form the Wado-ryu style of karate, which he characterized in the phrase, *ten-chi-jin, ri-do,* or "heaven-earth-man, principle way."

In later years, Yasuhiro Konishi, another senior disciple of Funakoshi, who also studied with Shuri-te master Choki Motobu in Okinawa,

Shotokan Karate: Its History and Evolution

Masatoshi Nakayama

founded the Shindo-jinen-ryu, while Kosei Kokuba (Kuniba) of Shito-ryu and Teruo Hayashi, a modern-day master of the Kenshin-ryu, founded their own schools, until today there are at least 75 styles of karate-do and 30 or more styles of karate-jutsu in Japan.

However, the four original styles—Shotokan, Goju, Wado and Shito—composed and continue to compose the bulk of Japanese karate. Unlike today, there was very little bickering or disagreement among the leaders of the various schools in Japan. It was perfectly acceptable, they believed, for different masters to teach in different ways; after all, they were all striving toward the same goal—perfection of human character through karate-do.

Partly because of the growing popularity of karate in Japan, it was during the period of 1930-1935 that Funakoshi's karate underwent the greatest changes.

Masatoshi Nakayama, one of the greatest masters produced during that period, later recalled:

> "(Originally) the training sessions under Master Funakoshi were very strict and rigid. During class sessions at the university, Funakoshi Sensei would have us perform technique after technique, hundreds of times each. When he selected a *kata* for us to practice, we would repeat it at least 50 or 60 times, and this was always fol-

lowed by intense practice on the *makiwara*. We would punch the *makiwara* until our knuckles were bloody. Master Funakoshi himself would join us at the *makiwara,* and I can vividly remember him striking the *makiwara* as many as 1,000 times with his elbows. The training was so grueling that of the 60 or so freshmen who enrolled with me in 1932, only six or seven of us made it through the first six months of training. The rest quit.

"My seniors...knew only *kata;* it was the only thing Master Funakoshi taught them. But in my generation, things began to change. The people in my generation were required to study martial arts beginning in grammar school, and continuing all the way through graduation from high school. Karate was not taught in the schools at that time, so all of us had studied judo or kendo. I began kendo training in grammar school, for example, and my friends had also practiced for a long time. But judo and kendo were centered around combat—throwing an opponent or actually striking an opponent with a sword. So, the idea of combat was deeply ingrained in us, and we really needed the combative aspect that karate lacked. Master Funakoshi understood this, and he began to change his teaching methods to meet the needs of our younger generation.

"We needed more than just *kata* all the time, and he realized that things would have to change if he was going to attract young people and see his art grow. So, he picked techniques from the *kata* and began teaching *gohon kumite* (five-step sparring) based on individual *kata* techniques. We would step in five times with the same attack while the defender blocked. Then the defender would counterattack. But we had high spirits, and if the defender did not counterattack immediately, we would attack him again, and he would be forced to improvise a defense and try to counter again. These actions became the basis for free-sparring. It was just a natural outgrowth of spirited young people practicing with one another. Shortly thereafter, we began *kihon-ippon kumite,* or one-step sparring. In this method, the attacker would announce the target area to be attacked, face or stomach, and would then execute his strongest, most powerful technique. The defender had only one chance to make a powerful, correct block and counterattack. This was very much in keeping with the basic philosophy of martial art, which revolves around the concept that there is no second chance. Everything must be done correctly the first time, or the person dies. We weren't trying to kill each other, of course, but we were trying to execute that one, perfect technique that would stop the opponent in a real fighting situation. A natural outgrowth of this kind of training was *jyu-ippon kumite* (semi-free, one-step sparring), in which the defender knew the area to be attacked, but in which the attacker could maneuver freely for position and distancing. The significant thing about this is that this was the first time karate had been taught in any way except for the application of *kata* movements to self-defense, and the entire system of *kumite* (sparring) developed in a single, five-year period. When Master Funakoshi published *Karate-do Kyohan (The Master Text of Karate-do)* in 1936, he included basic sparring methods in the book, and this was the first time this brand-new idea was introduced to the public at large.

Karate Comes to Japan

> "Also in this period came the idea of practicing each technique by itself, as we do today. Master Funakoshi felt that we should practice each technique independently to develop the feeling of *ikken hisatsu* (to stop the opponent with one blow) in our sparring. So we started practicing each technique by itself, marching up and down the floor, repeating the technique again and again. This is today the fundamental method of basic training. During my first five years in college, karate training was divided into the three main aspects we know today—*kihon* (basic training), *kata,* and *kumite.*
>
> "I began training in 1932, and basic *kumite* was introduced in 1933. In 1934, *jyu-ippon kumite* was introduced, and *jyu kumite* (free sparring) began in 1935."[2]

In November 1936, the All Japan Collegiate Karate Union was formed, and Nakayama joined Funakoshi in giving a demonstration at the Tokyo Civic Center. For the first time, the public was able to see how a karate student progresses from five-step sparring to one-step, semi-free, and free-sparring.

In 1935, karate men from all over Japan joined forces to pay Funakoshi a great accolade for his tireless work in introducing karate to Japan: They formed a committee that solicited funds to build the world's first, free-standing karate dojo.

According to Masatoshi Nakayama, this was no small matter:

> "At that time, we didn't have a karate dojo. Master Funakoshi was teaching in colleges, and he was teaching private groups from companies and the Tokyo Bar Association. A number of us, however, wanted more training than was available in college, so we would get together in the evenings

Gichin Funakoshi (front row, third from left) in 1935. In the front row, second from right, is his son, Yoshitaka. (From the original edition of Karate-do Kyohan)

and go to Master Funakoshi's house for more training at night.

"At the university, we would train for two hours at noon, and then we would go to Master Funakoshi's house in the evening for three more hours of training. At his house, Master Funakoshi had a wooden deck, which was really just a stairway with a little porch. While we trained, Master Funakoshi and his son, Yoshitaka, would sit on the floor on one end of the area and teach us. This was a very old method of teaching, and it was believed that the sensei could more fully concentrate on the movements of the students by sitting still and concentrating deeply.

"From time to time, Master Funakoshi would stand up and demonstrate a technique or explain a particular point, and then sit down again. I remember him sitting there with his back very straight and rigid, and often he would remain in that position for a full three hours, moving only when he wanted to show us some detail.

"The deck at Master Funakoshi's house was so small that only a couple of us could practice at one time, and since we often trained until after dark, we would frequently bump into one another. Of course, at this time, Master Funakoshi was not at all a wealthy man, so all of the students pooled our money and donated it to Master Funakoshi so he could expand his stairway, and that helped a great deal.

Gichin Funakoshi (left) in 1935 with his most senior student, Kichinosuke Saigo

"(The first public dojo) was built through the efforts of (Master Funakoshi's) students. His most senior student was Kichinosuke Saigo, a famous political figure in Japan, and Mr. Saigo organized a committee to solicit donations for the construction of a dojo. This marked the building of the first karate dojo in Japan."[3]

Construction on the building in Zoshigaya, Toshima Ward, began in mid-1938, and was completed in early 1939. Thus it was that Gichin Funakoshi, at the age of 71, bowed and entered the world's first karate dojo on January 29, 1939. As a tribute to him from karate students all over Japan, a plaque was hung over the door inscribed with the characters for "Shotokan," ("the hall of Shoto"). His students had used the pen name by which he signed his poetry to forever honor the man and his spirit.

According to Masatoshi Nakayama, both Funakoshi and his students were also conscious of the value of good public relations:

> "My feeling is that the development of Shotokan karate followed a special and very lucky developmental path. All of Master Funakoshi's early efforts were directed toward the teaching of the intelligentsia in Japan—doctors, lawyers, scholars, and artists. These people approached the art very seriously and from a high point of view. They studied hard and became very good, and they formed a very elite corps of senior students to represent Master Funakoshi's karate-do. So, when the dojo opened to the public, the public in general had the feeling that the art was an art of virtuous and important people. These seniors did not teach the general public, and I think this served to set them apart in the public eye as a very special group of important karate people. By keeping them separate from the general public, Master Funakoshi was able to use them as a strong base—an important group of people in the public eye, thoroughly grounded in the basics and philosophy of his

karate-do. The general students who came in to train thus had a very high ideal to look up to, and we always encouraged them to emulate Master Funakoshi's older students. This really helped to set Master Funakoshi's Shotokan karate-do apart from other styles in the public eye, and there is no doubt that it was a major contributing factor in the development of our large, international organization."[4]

It was in 1935 and 1936 that Funakoshi first actually acknowledged his position as undisputed leader of the karate movement in Japan. In what was for him a very courageous and revolutionary step, he suggested, first in newspaper articles and later in his book, *Karate-do Kyohan,* that karate had in fact become a pure Japanese martial art and should be accorded the same respect paid to kendo, judo, and other "pure" Japanese martial arts.

Shotokan-Karate-do

In this modern age of nomenclature and doublespeak, it is difficult to grasp the overwhelming audacity it took in 1936 Japan to first of all suggest that something as foreign as karate should be considered Japanese, and secondly to propose that the characters that had represented karate as Chinese throughout all of written history should be changed to different characters representing something entirely different.

What Funakoshi said, in effect, was that because many of the techniques had been introduced to Okinawa by Chinese merchants and seamen, the Okinawans had jumped at the chance to call the art Chinese. Up until about 1900, it was highly fashionable in Okinawa to have anything or do anything associated with the Chinese. Thus, the character commonly used for *kara* meant *"T'ang"* and referred to the T'ang dynasty of China. But, Funakoshi reasoned, the art was clearly Okinawan in nature and had now become clearly Japanese in nature. He therefore chose another character for *kara,* one which is also pronounced *ku,* and which is drawn from the Zen tradition.

In the Zen sense, *kara* means "emptiness" or "rendering oneself empty." Citing maxims from the Buddhist Prajnaparamita sutra, the *Hannya Shingyo,* such as *shiki-soku-ze-ku* ("form is emptiness") and *ku-soku-zeshiki* ("emptiness is form"), Funakoshi pointed out that *ku* (also pronounced *kara*) represented truth itself. This, he believed, more correctly represented the true nature of karate-do as a method of developing perfection in human character, and he proposed to the Keio University Karate Research Group that the art be renamed *Dai Nippon Kempo Karate-do* ("Great Japan Fist Method Empty-hands Way"), with *kara* written as "empty" rather than "Chinese."

For months after his initial article, letters and articles flew back and forth between disgruntled karate teachers and newspapers and magazines. Some of the masters on Okinawa were so shocked and offended that they never forgave Funakoshi for what they considered a betrayal, but most of them came to accept his idea within two years.

Regardless of the temporary flap, Funakoshi published *Karate-do Kyohan* in 1936 with the new characters replacing the old, and his will prevailed. From that moment forward, the "techniques of Chinese hands" became karate-do, "the way of the empty hand."

Karate Comes to Japan

The Shotokan Tiger
Hoan Kosugi, a famous artist and president of the Tabata Poplar Club, an artists' guild, was a very important figure in the development of Shotokan karate-do in Japan. It was Hoan Kosugi who, along with Jigoro Kano, was the most influential person in encouraging Gichin Funakoshi to teach karate in Japan in 1922.

As part of his enticement of Funakoshi, Hoan Kosugi told Funakoshi that if he would write a book about karate, he, Kosugi, would design it and provide a painting for the cover. When Gichin Funakoshi produced the book, Hoan Kosugi produced the now famous Shotokan tiger.

His idea for the tiger came from the expression, *"Tora no maki." Tora no maki,* in Japanese tradition, is the official written document of an art or system, which is used as the definitive reference source for that particular art. Since no books had ever been written about karate, Hoan Kosugi told Funakoshi that his book was the *tora no maki* of karate, and since *tora* also is the pronunciation of the *kanji* for "tiger," he designed the tiger, in a clever play on words, as a representation of Funakoshi's art.

4
The Japan Karate Association:
Karate for the Rest of the World

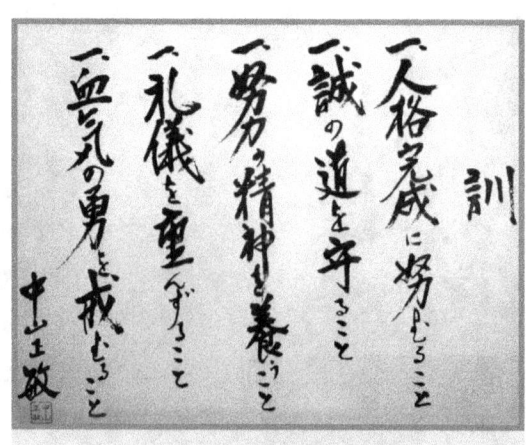

Dojo Kun calligraphy by Masatoshi Nakayama

By 1940, with Japan engaged in war on several fronts, Funakoshi's dojo was filled with eager young men training very hard. University clubs proliferated, and the old man's time was taken up entirely with the teaching of karate.

Following the Japanese attack on Pearl Harbor in 1941, Funakoshi's dojo was so crowded with students that they frequently spilled over onto the street and into neighboring yards. As the war in the Pacific dragged on, however, more and more of the young men were called to duty in the armed forces, and some of the most promising karate students were lost in battle.

In the Spring of 1945, Funakoshi's son, Giko (Yoshitaka), suffering from tuberculosis, was hospitalized. With his son gravely ill and unable to help him (Giko was a brilliant karate man) and the country under extreme pressure from American bombers, Funakoshi moved in with his eldest son in Koishikawa.

While living there, the first of two great successive tragedies struck Funakoshi. His cherished dojo, the living monument dedicated to him by his students and admirers, was completely destroyed in an air raid. Shortly thereafter, Giko, the promising young karate master who was destined to carry on his father's work and tradition, died.

Seeing everything he had worked for laying in ruin, Funakoshi made a renewed effort to bring his wife to Japan to be with him. For all the many years he had spent in Tokyo, she had remained in Okinawa, raising their family and taking care of the elders. Now, with the family raised and Okinawa under siege, she finally agreed to join her husband, and they were reunited in Oita in Kyushu. Remaining in the country where they could eke out an existence on the war-torn land, they lived together until 1947. In the late fall of that year, Funakoshi's wife died.

Encouraged by his son to return to Tokyo, Funakoshi carried his wife's ashes with him on the long train journey, and, much to his surprise, his former students were gathered at every stop to express their condolences and respect.

Encouraged by the return of many of his students from the war, Funakoshi embarked upon a rebuilding project for karate in 1947. As will be discussed later, this led to the establishment of the Nihon Karate Kyokai (Japan Karate Association) beginning in May 1949.

In 1953, the U.S. government prevailed upon Funakoshi to demonstrate karate for members of the Strategic Air Command

The Japan Karate Association

(SAC) at several Far Eastern bases. At the age of 83, this remarkable man boarded a U.S. government plane and, accompanied by Masatoshi Nakayama of Takushoku University, Toshio Kamata of Waseda University, and Isao Obata of Keio University, toured many U.S. air bases and demonstrated karate to thousands of members of SAC. From July to December of that

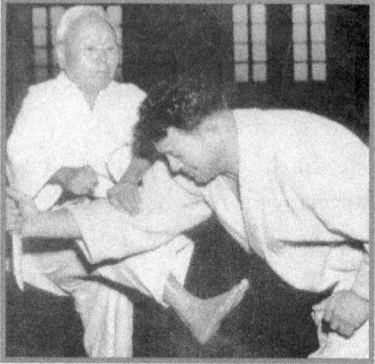

Gichin Funakoshi demonstrates knife defense against Mel Bruno, founder of the SAC martial arts program.

Some of Japan's leading martial artists are greeted during their SAC tour at Offut Air Force Base in Omaha, Nebraska. Second from left is Hidetaka Nishiyama. Sixth from left (behind officer) is Kenji Tomiki, founder of one of the major schools of aikido. Third from right is Isao Obata, founder of the Shotokai. Shaking hands with the officer is Sumiyaki Kotani, then chief instructor of Kodokan judo.

year, he supervised an extended tour of SAC bases in the United States, sending Obata, Kamata and Hidetaka Nishiyama.

Forever tireless, Funakoshi wrote in 1956 that his next great goal was to see the internationalization of true karate-do. He did not live to see his final dream fulfilled, but it was a dream carried to fulfillment by his students and successors.

Gichin Funakoshi was a man of extraordinary vision and energy—a man who, through the force of his intellect, personality, and tenacity, rose to the challenges presented him and sought more.

(Left to Right) Masatoshi Nakayama, Isao Obata, Hidetaka Nishiyama, and Mel Bruno

Hidetaka Nishiyama, reminiscing in 1978, ascribed the whole of karate development to the intrinsic personality characteristics of the man.

According to Nishiyama:

> "(Master Funakoshi's) instructions usually took the form of explanations of the philosophy of

the technique we were practicing, or an interesting story about famous Okinawan martial arts masters who had developed the technique. This helped the students a great deal and gave us the foundations of our techniques as a martial art. I think Master Funakoshi's personality, more than anything else, influenced our thinking about what karate is and should be. And it is due to his personality that karate has grown to its present state."[1]

When Gichin Funakoshi died on April 26, 1957, he took with him forever the unifying force of karate-do, and the progress of Shotokan karate-do since then has followed a somewhat different course from what the master might have envisioned.

Master Funakoshi's successors have changed some things around a bit to help fit the art into foreign cultures, but their changes have not been nearly so radical as some of their detractors sometimes claim. Their innovations have been in keeping with the master's actions in changing the names of the kata to make them more intelligible to the Japanese.

Even the Okinawan masters, who were less than pleased with their "secret" art being exported to the Japanese, did not question the necessity and efficacy of making minor changes for the sake of communication and adaptation.

From his first day in Japan, Funakoshi clearly perceived that the introduction and growth of his art would proceed most successfully within the social structure of the upper classes—scholars, lawyers, college teachers, military men—and it would have been unthinkable and also foolish to expect these people to cling to the terminology and structure of what they generally considered to be a plebeian culture. Further, as an educator, he was intent on seeing karate accepted as a physical education program in the schools, and he felt simplicity of both technique and nomenclature would be beneficial.

He therefore moved immediately to rename the *kata*. Of the

15 fundamental *kata* he took to Japan, only Jutte ("ten hands") and Jion (a proper name), retained their original names. The five Pinan kata were renumbered and modified by Funakoshi, primarily on the earlier advice of their inventor, Yasutsune Itosu, and appeared in Japan as Heian ("Peaceful"); the three Naihanchi emerged as Tekki ("Iron Horse" or "Horse Riding"); Patasai became Bassai ("To Penetrate a Fortress"); Koshokun evolved into Kushanku, then Kwanku, and finally Kanku ("Sky Viewing"); Wanshu became Empi ("Flying Swallow"); Seichin was changed to Hangetsu ("Crescent" or "Half Moon") and Chinto appeared as Gankaku ("Crane on a Rock"). Of the miscellaneous kata practiced more after Funakoshi's death, some have been renamed (Rohai, for example, is now called Meikyo), and some have not (Gojushiho, Nijushiho, Unsu and others). While all these changes may seem radical today, they were merely common sense necessities when they occurred.

Indeed, in 1982 Masatoshi Nakayama was emphatic on the matter of changes in karate-do:

> "Today the JKA follows Master Funakoshi's method exactly. We do constantly research to try to find ways to make the body stronger and the techniques stronger, but we follow Master Funakoshi's methods exactly.
>
> "We have not changed a single basic principle in all these years. What we have found through our research is that, by and large, Master Funakoshi's basic principles are correct, strong, and valid in the light of scientific evidence. When I say that there have been changes, I mean that with the advent of tournament competition, we have found it necessary to change the manner in which some techniques are applied for the specific application to competition. But basics are basics, and we have not changed them.

The Japan Karate Association

"Some individuals have initiated changes, but their actions are wrong and unacceptable. Some people, for example, have gotten the mistaken notion that competition is everything, and they train with the sole purpose of winning the competition. This is absolutely wrong. Master Funakoshi's karate rests on the foundation of developing strong basic techniques first, through *kihon* and *kata,* and then using *kumite* to test the techniques against one another. Any other approach is not in keeping with his principles.

"You see, before Master Funakoshi died, I began researching the idea of developing tournament, or sport karate. But when I asked Master Funakoshi for advice, he refused to comment. He was worried, you see, that if the tournament concept became too popular, then students would get away from the basic principles and practice only for tournament competition. He knew we would have karate tournaments and that they would be important for internationalizing karate, but he wanted it clearly understood that the most important thing would always be the basic training first.

"Change is natural, but it must occur correctly. For example, the precise origins of many of the *kata* are lost in the mists of history. However, to take one example, the *kata* we now call Kanku Dai was formerly called Kushanku, and we practice it exactly the way Master Funakoshi interpreted it. But it derives from a form originally called Koshokun, and it is believed that this *kata* was taught to many Okinawans by a Chinese attaché. Many, many people learned this *kata* and then went their separate ways, developing and studying their own arts. Over time, they changed the basic form of the *kata* to suit the needs of their particular style or particular body structure or particular individual needs. Consequently, there were, and are now, many different forms of the *kata*, Koshokun.

"The same is true of Bassai Dai. There are even more versions of Bassai than there are of Koshokun. The famous master, Matsumura, was noted for his practice and development of Bassai, and many people learned the *kata* from him. Again, these individuals in many cases changed the *kata* to suit their own needs, and today the number of different versions of Bassai is probably in the hundreds. But Master Funakoshi chose the form of the *kata* that he felt was the most effective, and we practice that form of the *kata*. So, the *kata* we call Kanku Sho and Bassai Sho are simply well-known variations of the original *kata*, Kanku and Bassai.

"The way they came to be practiced among Master Funakoshi's students is not really a matter of deeper meaning or significance. It is a matter of human nature. Some of the older students, chief among them being Master Funakoshi's son, Yoshitaka, would, from time to time, practice some of these versions they had learned elsewhere, and the younger students would be fascinated. We would imitate our seniors and ask them to teach us these differ-

Yoshitaka Funakoshi

ent forms. They would teach us, but then they would always say, 'There is nothing wrong with practicing another form, but remember that you must always concentrate on mastering the 15 basic forms. They are all you need to fully master karate, and you must not neglect them.'

"A *kata* developed by Yoshitaka Sensei, for example, is Sochin. Sochin was his specialty, and we learned it from him, but it is not one of the essential 15 *kata*.

"Master Funakoshi probably considered our desire to learn these other *kata* as youthful exuberance, but there was no harm in picking up different ideas from different *kata*. It is useful, but not, according to Master Funakoshi, essential.

"Some of the *kata* have come into the JKA system because Master Funakoshi took me around Japan to visit and pay courtesy calls on some of the other old masters in Osaka, Kyoto, Okuyama, and Hiroshima. We would exchange ideas with these masters, and they were, of course, anxious to learn Master Funakoshi's *kata*. In one instance, I remember we visited the founder of Shito-ryu, Kenwa Mabuni. Well, Master Funakoshi had already studied the goju and shito styles of karate and had incorporated the basic elements of these styles into Shotokan. The *kata* Hangetsu, for example, is essentially a goju style *kata*. If one practices Hangetsu, it is very easy to then exercise the goju *kata*, Tensho and Sanchin. Gankaku and Empi, on the other hand, are essentially Shorin style *kata*. But Master Funakoshi never ceased his study of other forms of karate, and when we visited Master Mabuni, Master Funakoshi told me to learn Mabuni's versions of Gojushiho and

Nijushiho so we could study them more carefully. So Kenwa Mabuni taught me his versions of these *kata*. Just as a natural outgrowth of our study of these *kata*, the *kata* eventually changed their form to conform to the form of movement of Shotokan karate, and they are now practiced by many of our members.

"But the most important thing I want to say about all of this is that I consider myself to be one of the luckiest human beings alive. I was so lucky to train under Master Funakoshi! His genius lay in his deep wisdom and judgment. He literally created Shotokan karate from the elements of all the different styles of karate in existence. Shotokan contains elements of both Goju-ryu and Shito-ryu, and if a person devotes himself to the mastery of Master Funakoshi's 15 *kata*, he will be able to easily pick up the essence of any other style of karate. Master Funakoshi was looking to the future when he created Shotokan—looking toward the day when all of karate would be united into one—and we will always be indebted to him for his work."[2]

What occupied Funakoshi most throughout the 1920s and 1930s was the development of collegiate karate until, by 1940, more than 30 percent of the colleges and universities in Japan had official karate clubs operating under the auspices of the one of the four major styles.

Additionally, each university had a so-called "Old Boys" club which was composed of karate men who were alumni of the school. The Old Boys stayed to themselves during training time, and they exerted a great deal of influence over the course of karate training at their various schools. They usually had office space on campus, and they would visit the regular classes to make sure training was being conducted properly. With so much prestige

The Japan Karate Association

afforded the Old Boys, the university clubs developed a great deal of pride, each seeking to be better than rival universities.

Japan's defeat in World War II, of course, brought to a temporary halt the development of virtually all the martial arts, but for Funakoshi's karate, this halt was short-lived. Almost immediately after the war, the karate men began reorganizing, with their goal being to build a large, strong karate organization as a tribute to their teacher, Funakoshi.

Masatoshi Nakayama had spent the war years in China, and had continued daily karate practice there. Upon returning to Tokyo in 1946, he discovered that his experiences in China had prepared him to lead the reorganization of karate in Japan:

> "I spent a great deal of time in China, and my experiences there strongly influenced my thinking about martial arts. At Takushoku University in Tokyo, I was majoring in Chinese history and language (Mandarin), and I planned a trip to China in my sophomore year. The trip took on more significance for me because of an incident that occurred in the Spring of my freshman year. I had been training in karate for several months by that time, and some friends and I went out to the country for a flower viewing picnic. While we were minding our own business, some ruffians started giving us trouble, and I was very quick to show them the power of karate kicks and punches. I was very proud of being able to defend myself and my friends, but when Master Funakoshi heard about it, he was furious. He severely reprimanded me. He told me that I had good physical skills, but that I was emotionally and spiritually immature. He said that my actions were those of a coward and an immature child, and that true courage lies in self-restraint and self-discipline. It took much more

courage, he said, to walk away when confronted with trouble than it did to just start punching and kicking everybody in sight.

"His words had a profound effect on me, and I determined to make my trip to China a search for spiritual maturity. So, from June to September of my sophomore year, I traveled on foot through Manchuria, across the Greater Khingan Mountains, into Outer Mongolia. I practiced karate every day, but I was really lonely, afraid, and usually hungry. But in that vast solitude of Outer Mongolia, I think I began to grasp the essence of self-confidence and self-reliance. It helped me to see more clearly into my own nature, and I was able, for the most part, to overcome my loneliness and fear.

"In 1937, I went to Peking as an exchange student to continue my study of Chinese language, society and history. And wouldn't you know it! One of the first things I saw in China was Chinese boxing! At first, I wasn't very impressed with the Chinese arts. They emphasized circular movements, and they had no *kime* (focus) like Japanese karate, so I thought they were weak.

"As time went by, though, I learned that the Chinese arts had a lot of value. The history of China is long and deep, and so is the history of her martial arts. I once saw an instructor receive a broken arm from what appeared to be a soft, circular block, and I decided that I must look deeper into the Chinese martial arts, so I began studying them, and continued studying them for almost 10 years.

"I trained very hard with many different instructors, and since I was also teaching karate, an art they had never seen, many of the instructors got to know me fairly well. In fact, when a

The Japan Karate Association

Japanese newspaper sent a film crew to do a story about Chinese martial arts, *sifu* (teachers) from all over China came to demonstrate for the cameras, and they asked me to act as their interpreter. As a courtesy to me, they also insisted that I demonstrate karate, so I did. In my demonstration, I emphasized *kime* and *kata*.

"At this time, Japan and China were on the verge of war, and it was rather disconcerting to see the Japanese and Chinese newspapers squabbling over which country had the best martial arts. The Japanese said that Chinese boxing looked pretty, but lacked speed and *kime,* and was obviously no good for fighting. The Chinese retorted that while karate appeared to be fast and strong and extremely powerful, it was still just a brand-new martial art and lacked refinement and depth. Since I was teaching karate to a lot of sincere Chinese students and they were teaching me kung fu and tai chi, we found the whole affair amusing.

"My own feeling was, and is, that while karate techniques rely on conservation of energy, which is released all at once at the end of a technique like an explosion, the Chinese arts waste a lot of energy in preparatory movements and deliver their power like the slow sweep of a sword. But my training in China deeply impressed on me the idea that two cultures, so different on the outside, could both independently develop effective martial arts based on their individual cultures and rooted deeply in the same philosophical base—the philosophy of human beings seeking perfection of character through physical expression. That, to me, is the most important thing.

"And please don't misunderstand; I'm not saying that Chinese martial arts are bad. I trained for a long time with an 80-year-old *sifu* named Pai—a famous Peking boxer—who was absolutely extraordinary with his legs. He seemed to be able to wrap his leg around an attacking arm, and his defensive movements were marvelous. As a result of studying with him, I developed two new kicks that were incorporated into karate techniques by Master Funakoshi when I returned to Japan. One is a pushing kick or block using the sole of the foot or the lower portion of the leg, and the other is the reverse roundhouse kick.

"I spent five years at the university in Peking, and several more working for the Chinese government.

"When I returned to Tokyo in 1946, I found that conditions in the country were terrible! I had naively thought I could get a job teaching Chinese, but the whole country was immersed in reconstruction after the war, and there were very few academic jobs available. I worked as a dry goods salesman for a while to support myself.

"One of the first things I did upon my return to Tokyo was to begin looking up my old comrades and karate seniors. But so many of them had been lost in the war! Those who remained were not active in karate, for the most part. So I immediately moved to get us all together and start training again. I was fortunate, of course, because I had continued regular training during my years in China.

"It was against the law to practice martial arts in Japan after the war, but the edict of GHQ (General Headquarters of Allied Powers) was worded in such a way that it included karate as a part of judo. I had a friend who knew the head of

The Japan Karate Association

the Education Bureau at the Ministry of Education, and he helped us convince the allied powers that karate was not part of judo at all. Using the premise that karate was actually a form of Chinese boxing—a sport—we received permission to practice. The GHQ thought karate was just a harmless pastime! So, while the other martial arts had to wait until the ban was lifted in 1948, we were able to practice and progress."[3]

In May 1949, Funakoshi's students—the university clubs, the Old Boys clubs, and the private dojo all over Japan—loosely organized themselves into the Nihon Karate Kyokai (Japan Karate Association, commonly called the JKA), and named Funakoshi their Chief Instructor Emeritus.

A 1952 photo taken at a special exhibition for the National Railroad Company of Japan. Seated at far left is Gichin Funakoshi. Standing behind him (left to right) is Masatoshi Nakayama (in gi); Masatomo Takagi, founder of Takushoku University Karate Club; Iso Obata, founder of Keio University Karate Club; Hiroshi Noguchi, founder of Waseda University Karate Club; Hidetaka Nishiyama, senior from Takushoku; and Mr. Endo, senior from Waseda. In the fourth row (wearing gi) are Toshio Yanase and Motokuni Sugiura; and Teruyuki Okazaki, Mamoru Onoue, and Toshio Irie, all Takushoku seniors.

Virtually all of the senior instructors had just returned from outside the country following the war, and they had no capital to invest in building a dojo. The JKA functioned without a dojo, in fact, until 1955. During the period 1949-1955, the organization used the facilities of the various university clubs for training.

In 1954, Masatomo Takagi, later Vice Chairman of the JKA, was lamenting to his former college roommate about the desire everyone had to build another dojo in tribute to Master Funakoshi.

His friend was the younger brother of a man who owned a large piece of ground in the Yotsuya section of Tokyo. Takagi's friend told him that his brother was a movie maker who was interested in the artistic qualities of *budo* and who was also considering building a movie studio at Yotsuya.

Masatomo Takagi in his JKA office in the early 1960s.

Several conversations later, the older brother agreed to include a complete dojo in his building plans for Yotsuya. Opened in April, 1955, the Yotsuya dojo became the permanent home of the JKA until the early 1970s, at which time a huge dojo was opened in Ebisu.

Organizationally, the JKA was set up along regional lines, and in 1959 gained the official recognition of the Ministry of Education as Japan's official karate organization. Primarily, it was composed of the Old Boys and university clubs of Hosei, Keio, Takushoku, and Waseda Universities.

Of the three principal regions, the Kanto (Tokyo) Region was

The Japan Karate Association

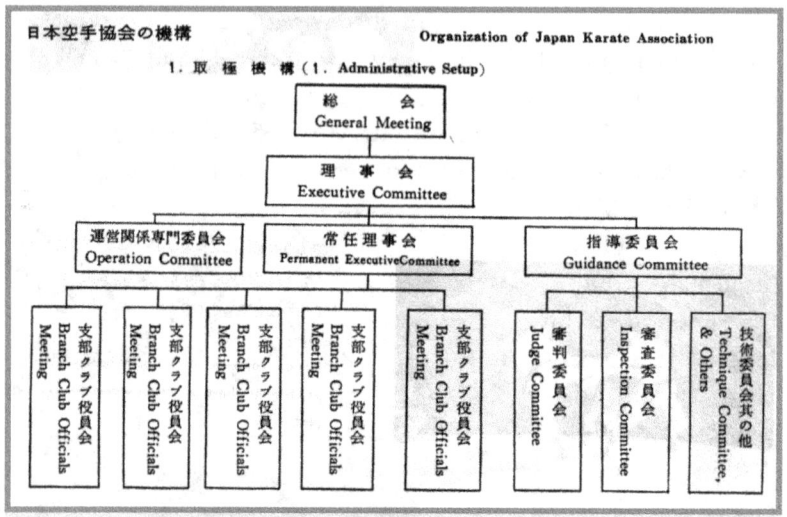

The administrative structure of the Japan Karate Association in 1960
(From the JKA's first official public brochure)

Minoru Miyata (L)

Osamu Ozawa

administered directly by the headquarters staff, while the Hokkaido (northern island) Region headed by Minoru Miyata, and the Kansai (Osaka, Kobe and Kyoto) Region headed by

Osamu Ozawa, were administered by Old Boys clubs from universities in the respective areas.

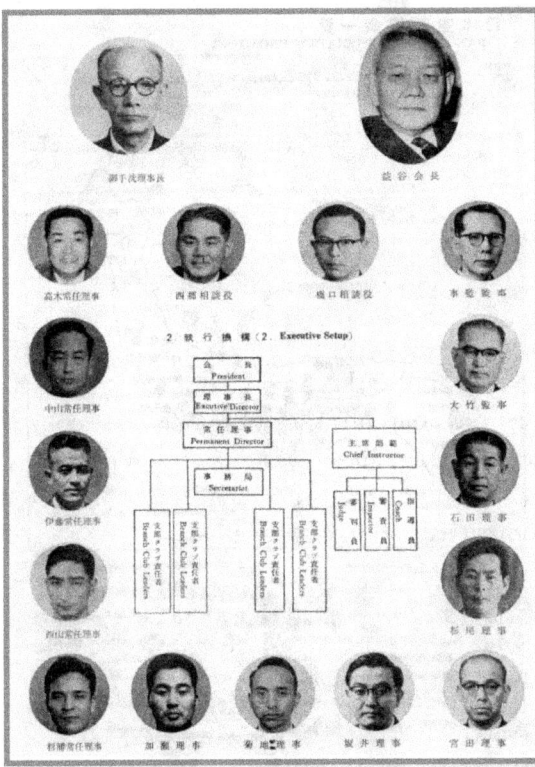

The executive branch structure of the
Japan Karate Association in 1960
(From the JKA's first official public brochure)

The JKA was originally organized by a number of very influential (and, more often than not, wealthy) people. Isao Obata, the Chairman, was the wealthy President of his own trading company; the first JKA President, Kichinosuke Saigo, was a wealthy politician with major political influence. However, these men had neither the time nor the inclination to administer the affairs of such a large and burgeoning organization, and the Board of Directors immediately hired a full-time paid staff to run the organization.

With Japan still not fully recovered from World War II, it was relatively easy to find unemployed, extraordinarily talented people who had both administrative skills and karate expertise. Masatomo Takagi, a very talented business manager and a fifth dan (fifth degree black belt) in karate, was hired as General Secretary.

The Japan Karate Association

Masatoshi Nakayama was appointed Chief Instructor to conduct the day-to-day training at the headquarters; Kimio Itoh was appointed Director of Administration; and Hidetaka Nishiyama, a legend in his own time in collegiate karate, was appointed Chief of the Instruction Committee.

Kimio Itoh referees a match between Ray Dalke of the U.S. and Andy Sherry of Great Britain.

At first glance, it would appear that an organization with such highly qualified teachers and administrators would be successful beyond anyone's wildest fantasies, and it was to a certain degree, but not without severe difficulties, the consequences of which set the course for the internationalization of karate.

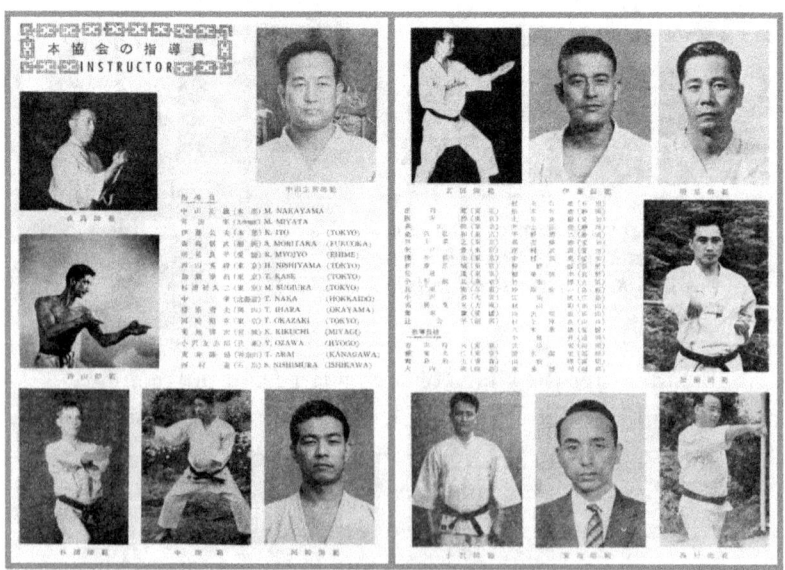

**Official instructors of the JKA in Japan in 1960
(From the JKA's first official public brochure)**

Central to an understanding of what happened to the JKA and its export of karate to the rest of the world is a clear perception of the pre-World War II rigid class structure of Japan. Both ancestry and wealth contributed to a man's position along class lines, and Japanese institutions, especially the colleges and universities, were designed accordingly. Even today, a family's wealth and position determine to a large degree which university the children will attend, and the graduate's chances for success are strongly influenced by which college he attended. With the exception of Gakashuin, which was originally for aristocrats, the "Big Three" colleges, in terms of social and political prestige, are Keio, Waseda, and Hosei. Graduates of these universities come from wealthy and influential families, and they have no difficulty finding positions with the largest companies and institutions. These three, along with Takushoku, also represented the best collegiate karate in Japan.

Takushoku, however, was not part of the "establishment" of colleges. Commonly called Takudai, it was established before World War II expressly for the purpose of producing trained administrators for overseas work. Takushoku literally means "cultivation and colonization." The Japanese felt they were building an empire on foreign soil, and would need trained administrators to oversee business in the colonies. Takudai men, therefore, typically majored in economics, importing and exporting, and international law. The types of jobs available to Takudai graduates were not considered prestigious by the old-line university graduates, and a good deal of class consciousness was evident in the JKA between the upper echelon Old Boys and highly expert (in karate) but "lower class" Takudai men. This tension inevitably manifested itself in disputes over business practices, philosophy, and training methods.

The class division problem among the administrators was compounded by the fact that the Takudai staff, such as Takagi and Nakayama, was being paid for teaching karate.

In April 1955, when the JKA opened its first commercial dojo in the preview room of the Kataoka Movie Center, a strong campaign was launched for the recruitment of new students. Many of

The Japan Karate Association

the old-line masters, chief among them being Isao Obata of Keio, felt it was immoral for a man to accept money for teaching the art. Even those who would not deny a man the right to be paid voiced strong opposition to the concept of placing karate on the market as a consumer product. When the student is paying the instructor, they believed, the instructor cannot teach as well as he could if no money were involved.

Masatoshi Nakayama

There were undoubtedly many other factors involved, not the least of which was the difference of opinion on instruction methods, but there is no doubt that these two factors—divisions along class lines and irreconcilable disputes over the proper student-teacher relationship—contributed in large measure to the departure of some of the major Old Boys groups from the JKA.

The Hosei Old Boys were the first to go, followed by Obata and the Keio group. Without the restraints of the conservative Old Boys from the mainline universities, the Takudai men were now free to pursue the development of karate in their own way, and it is not surprising that they chose to internationalize karate with vigor; after all, their college backgrounds had prepared them specifically to conduct business overseas. And the main tool they selected to implement their overseas drive was "sport" karate.

While not exclusively the domain of the Takudai men, sport

karate developed primarily under their guidance and along their lines of thought. Their rationale was simply that the best way for an art like karate to gain attention and be accepted internationally was for it to have a sporting aspect. This, it might be added, did nothing to improve their image in the eyes of the dissident Old Boys, most of whom fervently clung to the concept of karate-do as a personal martial art that could only be denigrated by sport.

The idea of turning karate into a sport with rules for competition was not new or unique. Since 1936, college clubs had been conducting kokangeiko ("exchange of courtesies and practice"), in which they tested their techniques against each other on a freestyle basis. Without formal rules or supervision, however, these "exchange training" sessions were, more often than not, fist fights using the techniques of karate. A less polite, but equally accurate, term would be "bloodbaths."

"These exchanges were supposed to consist of *kata* practice and one-step sparring with prearranged attacks and defenses," Masatoshi Nakayama would say years later. "In reality, they often degenerated into brawls. I saw broken noses and jaws, teeth knocked out, and ears almost ripped off."

Many of the Old Boys tacitly refused to acknowledge the existence of such shenanigans, first because they disapproved of free-sparring for sport, and second because they judged such actions to be in direct opposition to the basic principles of karate as Funakoshi taught them.

But Masatoshi Nakayama held another view:

> "I was torn between the belief that karate needed a combative aspect and the sure knowledge that someone was going to be killed if this sort of thing went unchecked. Especially in the pacifistic atmosphere of postwar Japan, I saw kendo and judo flourishing as sports, and I was concerned that if karate continued on its bloody course, the people would reject it."

The Japan Karate Association

With reasoning typical of his samurai heritage, Nakayama determined to maintain tradition by breaking tradition.

> "My solution was to study the rules of many different kinds of sports and to experiment with various ideas of competition. Once, for example, I set up matches in which contestants wore heavy padding and fought full-contact. The padding was designed on the order of kendo armor, but it was, of course, much lighter. To my great dismay, we found that the armor itself, because of its bulkiness and restriction of movement, caused more injuries than it prevented. Finally, the committee members and I came up with what we thought would be a viable set of rules for sparring.
>
> "...My greatest concern at that time was to ensure that karate, if given a sporting aspect, would not lose its essence as an art. I therefore worked very hard on designing *kata* competition, and I based the rules on the rules of skating and gymnastics competitions. My one hope was to preserve the essence of karate-do as an art of self-defense and self-denial, and to prevent the excitement of sparring from transforming karate into a mere sport."[4]

The JKA directors and others in other styles began bringing free sparring out into the open, experimenting with it, debating it, and, finally, encouraging it. By 1950, virtually all the major styles of karate in Japan were practicing some form of freestyle sparring. The problem of developing a set of rules was the biggest obstacle to overcome.

Hidetaka Nishiyama was at the center of the developmental problems, and years later described the major difficulties faced by the instructors who were trying to devise a workable formula for freestyle sparring rules:

Drawing inspiration from a karate tournament he attended, the renowned Japanese sculptor Hanazato in 1959 asked Hidetaka Nishiyama to pose for this bronze sculpture which was later exhibited nationally as part of the annual Japan National Arts Festival. The statue was displayed for years at the JKA headquarters dojo in Tokyo.

"The Japan Karate Association devoted over five years to devise a working set of tournament rules. During the period they not only discussed theoretical problems, but members of the committee were in the dojo...clad in their karate-gi... experimenting and exploring what was possible and (seeking) practical standards to formulate for both kumite and kata contests...

"The delay in the development of karate contests governed by rules was caused by several factors:

1. Karate has many techniques which are extraordinarily powerful and effective.

2. If actual contact is permitted, injury is unavoidable.

3. It is impossible to devise protective equipment which could withstand the impact of attacks coming from all angles.

4. Even if it were possible to devise such pro-

tective gear, it would not be useful from the standpoint of karate. Freedom of movement would be severely limited and it would hinder execution of precise techniques required of good karate.

5. Tests have demonstrated that the human neck cannot withstand the impact of a karate punch or kick to the face, even with a protective mask."5

But the JKA men were tenacious in their pursuit of what they knew would be the key element in internationalizing and popularizing karate. The JKA contest rules, comprising three chapters and 16 articles, were completed in August 1956.

All of the collegiate clubs and branch dojo immediately commenced staging tournaments, both for the development of contestant skills and for the training of judges.

This flurry of activity culminated in the staging of the first All Japan Karate-do Championship Tournament in June 1957. The Tokyo Metropolitan Gymnasium, the largest arena of its kind in Japan at that time, was jammed with spectators, and the face of karate, both in the public eye and in the eyes of its practitioners, was forever changed. The last dream of the little school teacher from Okinawa—to see karate accepted around the world-was about to become a reality.

Hirokazu Kanazawa (L) in the first All Japan Championship

Concurrent with their efforts to devise a workable set of

contest rules, the indefatigable JKA men instituted an incredibly rigid instructor training program for the development of instructors for overseas posts.

Masatoshi Nakayama's explanation of the rationale for the program sounds very much like the situation in modern America:

> "When Master Funakoshi first brought karate to Japan, he was the only one qualified to teach. Later, when Master Kenwa Mabuni brought Shito-ryu karate to Osaka, the art began to spread rapidly, and there were many, many students. This wide popularity led to the unfortunate situation in which individuals who had only six months of training under Master Funakoshi or Master Mabuni or someone else, started their own styles. By the time we organized the JKA and formed a corporation as an educational body under the Ministry of Education in 1955, there were about 200 so-called 'styles' of karate around. And the public had no way of knowing who was qualified to teach and who was not. It was therefore our task to establish standards for instruction and to register these standards with the Ministry of Education.
>
> "So, under Master Funakoshi's guidance, I began formulating the Instructor Training Program. My feeling was that ranking should not be the only criteria for appointing instructors. It was even more important to teach them how to teach others. They needed broad knowledge of other areas like physics, anatomy, psychology, management, and so on. But this was a monumental task, and I had to have the help and advice of the more senior students.
>
> "So, along with me, significant contributions were made to the program by Motokuni Sugiura,

The Japan Karate Association

Teruyuki Okazaki, Hidetaka Nishiyama, and other senior instructors."⁶

Only the very cream of the crop of young karate men were admitted to the program, and only after graduating honorably from college and attaining the second *dan* ranking. For a full year they would live in a dormitory and study karate from morning until night. Not only was their study physical, but they were prepared academically for their assignments with courses in psychology, physics, anatomy, business management, history and philosophy of physical education and sports, and myriad other technical subjects. Upon completion of the training program (which also required that they attain the third *dan* level and present a dissertation contributing something new and significant to karate instruction methods), they were assigned to a teaching internship for another full year. The result of this extraordinarily difficult apprenticeship was the production of a dozen or so of the most highly proficient karate men imaginable.

Teruyuki Okazaki

With near-fanatic dedication, these men and a few other high-ranking instructors launched their worldwide evangelistic campaign for karate and, to the chagrin and disgust of many in other styles, for the JKA in particular. Nothing, they had been taught, was bigger or more important than JKA karate-do and its correct transmission to the rest of the world, and this they believed completely, often to the detriment of others.

As a visionary on the future growth of karate, Gichin

Funakoshi was without peer. He clearly perceived that the world was ready for his art, and he spent the last decade of his life preparing for the export of karate to the rest of the world. During the period 1945-1954, he witnessed an increasing international interest in the art.

As early as 1948, Readers Digest carried an article mentioning the karate men of Japan, as did Mademoiselle magazine. Italy's national broadcasting company came to Japan and filmed a special feature on the art, and both the graduates of the SAC special training program and Japanese businessmen with interests overseas began spreading the word rapidly.

1958 photo marks the founders' meeting of what would become the Federation of All Japan Karate-do Organizations (FAJKO). Front row, left to right: Masters Ito, Yamaguchi, Ohtsuka, Takagi, and Ito (Shito-ryu)

At the same time, Funakoshi oversaw the production of two motion pictures designed to introduce karate to the rest of the world. The first, *Hien Karate-uchi,* was essentially a biographical film of Masatoshi Nakayama, and it played to packed houses all

The Japan Karate Association

over Asia. The other, *Karate-do,* was distributed worldwide in 16mm format with English narration. *Karate-do,* first issued in 1954, is still distributed popularly around the world. Funakoshi himself appears in this documentary film, and the techniques of karate are demonstrated by almost all of Funakoshi's first generation Japanese protégés.

Masatoshi Nakayama (L) and Teruyuki Okazaki (R) with their teacher, Gichin Funakoshi, on the grand opening day of the first JKA dojo in 1955.

In December 1954, the first formal export of karate to Asia, outside Japan, occurred in Thailand.

The Thai government, hearing many stories about karate, issued an invitation to instructors to demonstrate the art at the annual trade exhibition in Bangkok. Funakoshi sent Masatoshi Nakayama and Teruyuki Okazaki as cultural exchange delegates,

Members of the first graduating class of Boei University, Japan's West Point, pose in 1957 with their karate instructor, Teruyuki Okazaki (kneeling, in suit). To Okazaki's left is Yutaka Yaguchi, assistant instructor, and to Okazaki's right is Noriaki Tanaka, Boei Karate Team Captain, who would go on to become the Commander of the Army in Okinawa.

Hirokazu Kanazawa (left) and Takayuki Mikami at the end of the second All Japan Championship in 1958

The Japan Karate Association

both to demonstrate karate and to study the ancient art of Thai boxing. Originally scheduled for two weeks, their tour stretched to more than two months. During their two-month visit, Nakayama and Okazaki established a rudimentary training system for the police departments in various cities in Thailand, and set the stage for many more exchanges between the two countries, primarily in the form of exchange of techniques for use by law enforcement personnel.

By the time of his death in 1957, Funakoshi had seen the completion of the first instructor training program. In that year, the Far East University in the Philippines issued an official request for an instructor to teach karate as part of the regular academic curriculum. Takayuki Mikami, one of only three original graduates of the training program, was given the assignment, and he remained in the Philippines for two years, teaching karate on a fulltime basis. In 1958, Hirokazu Kanazawa, Mikami's classmate, accepted an invitation from Hawaii, and Shotokan karate began to flourish internationally under the auspices of the JKA.

Gichin Funakoshi in the early 1950s.

5
Karate Comes to the United States

Gichin Funakoshi brought karate to Japan in 1922, and the United States Air Force brought karate to the United States in 1953. Indeed, the first formal introduction of karate to the United States was arranged by the Strategic Air Command (SAC). Beginning in 1948, the U.S. Air Force arranged for a series of martial arts demonstrations at their bases at Tachikawa, Kisarazu, Tokorozawa, and Yokosuka. From 1948 through 1951, some of Japan's finest exponents of karate, judo, and kendo gave demonstrations twice a week at these air bases. The karate demonstrations usually were led by Isao Obata and Masatoshi Nakayama. American interest was so great that many airmen began seeking instruction, and soon karate and judo clubs were established on the bases.

The American interest in karate was by no means limited to Gichin Funakoshi's karate. Many American servicemen began training in earnest in many different styles, and this interest gave impetus to the Japanese to organize themselves more carefully.

In 1946, Doshin So systematized Shorinji-Kempo in Shikoku, Japan, and Kanken Toyama founded the All Japan Karate-do

Association, introducing his style, Shudokan, to numerous GIs. Back in Okinawa in 1947, Shoshin Nagamine founded the Matsubayashi Shorin-ryu, largely on the strength of the numerous American soldiers seeking his instruction.

In Japan in 1950, Chojiro Tani founded the Shukokai style of karate, and Gogen Yamaguchi officially organized the Karate-do Goju-Kai. The organizations founded by these masters eventually produced strong, large, international organizations, particularly in Europe. Even the small Koei-Kan style, founded by Eizo Onishi in 1952, enjoyed great popularity among American and British service personnel stationed in Japan during the occupation.

Nevertheless, it was the JKA men who officially organized and introduced Shotokan karate to America.

In 1951, SAC hired Emilio Bruno, a civilian judo man, to organize and direct a physical training program in the martial arts for SAC personnel. The theory behind this program was that the B-47 bomber (then America's main bomber) was essentially a short-range aircraft. In a global conflict, it was reasoned, the B-47 would not be capable of a roundtrip on a long-range mission, and the pilots would likely find themselves down in enemy territory. This would be both physically and mentally stressful, and it was felt that the martial arts, with their strong mental and physical discipline, would help the pilots in such circumstances.

Additionally, SAC was involved in a program that required many of its pilots to be in the air and on the ground in continuously rotating, 12-hour shifts. By practicing the martial arts, it was found, the pilots could fly for 12 hours, do the exercises, and be refreshed for their next flight.

Thus it was that 23 American airmen arrived at the Kodokan in 1951 for an intensive, eight-week training program in judo, karate, aikido, and taiho-jutsu (techniques of restraint).

This program was successful beyond anyone's expectations, and it continued for 15 years, with hundreds of American servicemen participating, many of them returning to Japan again and again to increase their skills and delve more deeply into the arts.

Karate Comes to the United States

A typical SAC training class at the Kodokan in the 1950s. First row, left, is Hidetaka Nishiyama. Second row, left, is Masatoshi Nakayama. Third row, left, is Shinkin Gima, standing next to Sumiyaki Kotani, Chief Instructor of the Kodokan. Fourth row, left, is Isao Obata, and fourth row, right is Emilio Bruno.

By 1953, it was apparent to the Air Force that the program was successful, and they decided to expand the concept of the program to selected bases in the United States. In June of that year, SAC sponsored a tour of the U.S. that lasted for over six months. Included in the tour group were 10 of the highest-ranking judo men in Japan, and three of the premier karate men from the JKA (Isao Obata, Toshio Kamata, and Hidetaka Nishiyama). Throughout the tour, the group would visit each air base for approximately four days. One or two of those days was usually devoted to demonstrations and teaching, and the other days were taken up with travel to nearby cities to give demonstrations for the civilian population.

Without question, these formal demonstrations under the auspices of SAC did more to alert the American public to the existence of traditional Japanese martial arts than did any other single event before or since.

Prior to the SAC tour, the only other widespread display of

anything resembling karate in the United States was a tour by Masutatsu Oyama, a Korean who had adopted Japan as his home, and who had trained in karate under Gogen Yamaguchi. Since Oyama toured the U.S. as a professional "bad guy" wrestler, his demonstrations of karate could hardly be considered serious demonstrations of an art designed to improve human character. Perhaps the major contribution of Oyama was that he tried to get the word, "karate," into the English language, but the announcers of his bouts, more often than not, described his techniques as "judo chops."

Regardless of Oyama's efforts, the teaching of karate to SAC personnel at the Kodokan was the real pivotal point in the history and development of the art in America and in the development of modern karate teaching methods.

Masatoshi Nakayama immediately recognized that karate could not be taught to the Americans in the same fashion as it was taught to the Japanese. Prior to 1951, the coaching method had been fairly simple; it revolved around the teaching and practice of *kihon* and *kata*. The students would imitate their instructors, and they were left to find insights for themselves. But the Americans were different.

First of all, they were all different in size, and what worked for a small man might not work for a larger one.

Second, the Americans displayed an irritating trait not thought of by the Japanese: the Americans always wanted to know "why." "Why should I stand like this?" "Why should I twist at the hips?" "Why this, and why not that?"

As a result of this American inquisition, Nakayama and his assistants threw themselves into an intense study of kinesiology, anatomy, psychology, and physics. They set out to learn the scientific principles behind their body motions to be better able to convey intelligent answers to the inquiring Americans.

According to Masatoshi Nakayama, the SAC program and the study it engendered in the Japanese is the focal point in the history of karate in America:

Karate Comes to the United States

"The history of American karate really revolves around the decision of the Strategic Air Command to teach martial arts to their personnel.

"(The SAC personnel studied) the various martial arts under the leading instructors in Japan. This program continued for 15 years, and it exposed a large number of Americans to correct principles of karate, judo, aikido, and other martial arts. Certainly the men who participated in this program had a significant impact on bringing karate to America.

"In retrospect, I think the biggest impact resulting from our association with the Americans was that we were forced to find ways to explain karate to non-Japanese people. It immediately became apparent to me and to Master Funakoshi that if we were going to teach Americans, we would have to provide a theoretical basis for our art. The Americans simply were not satisfied with blindly following like the Japanese. So, under Master Funakoshi's guidance, I began an intense study of kinetics, physiology, anatomy, and hygienics. We believed that with a thorough grounding in the scientific basis of body mechanics, we would find it easier to teach foreigners. We were right, and we also learned a great deal about our own practice of the art."[1]

In one sense, their intense efforts bore fruit. More and more Americans became involved in karate, and many of them were able to progress at a much faster rate than the Japanese who were trained in the traditional manner. In another sense, the emphasis on scientific analysis jeopardized the ancient traditions and placed the intrinsic values of the art in grave peril. Even today, the final judgment on this matter has not been rendered. That is, we still do not know if the traditional precepts of courtesy, sincerity, effort, etiquette, and self-control can survive in the rational, analytic atmosphere of America.

From 1953 through 1960, various forms of karate were introduced to the American public, and interest in the art began to grow.

The first person to teach what he called karate in the United States was Robert Trias, who introduced his art in Phoenix, Arizona, in 1948. In 1954, Edward Kaloudis, a disciple of Onishi's Koei-Kan system, began teaching on the East Coast. In 1955, Edmund Parker opened the first West Coast karate studio in Pasadena, California, and Tsutomu Ohshima, an exchange student from Waseda University, began teaching Shotokan karate in Los Angeles. In the following year, Ohshima founded Shotokan Karate of America in Los Angeles, and Jhoon Rhee began teaching the Korean version of karate, Tae Kwon Do, in San Marcos, Texas.

1957 saw the introduction of Wado-ryu karate in Tennessee by Cecil Patterson, and the opening of the first commercial dojo in the Midwest, in St. Louis, Missouri, by Goju-ryu practitioner Ed Cwiklowski. In the same year, Isshin-ryu (a modern Okinawan style) instructor Don Nagle began teaching his style of the art in Jacksonville, North Carolina.

The Okinawan karate/kung-fu style, Uechi-ryu, was introduced in Boston in 1958 by George Mattson, another serviceman trained during extended tours in Okinawa.

In 1959, Hiroshi Orito, a second *dan* exchange student from Keio University, began teaching Funakoshi's karate in New York, and Peter Urban, a student of Gogen Yamaguchi, began teaching the Goju-ryu style in Union City, New Jersey.

1960 was perhaps the biggest year for karate before the JKA officially arrived in America. In 1960, Yoshiaki Ajari introduced Wado-ryu in Hayward, California; Anthony Mirakian introduced Okinawan Goju-ryu in Watertown, Massachusetts; and S. Henry Cho opened the first Tae Kwon Do studio in New York. Also in that year, Steve Armstrong, who had learned his art in the service while stationed in Okinawa, began teaching the Okinawan Isshin-

Karate Comes to the United States

ryu style of karate in Tacoma, Washington.

Indeed, the 1960s saw the introduction of virtually all the major styles of karate to the United States, the last two of these being the Shito-ryu style, introduced by Fumio Demura in Santa Ana, California, in 1965, and the Chito-ryu style, officially founded as the U.S. Chito Kai by William Dometrich in 1967 in Covington, Kentucky.

Encouraged by the early interest of the Americans in Japan during the occupation, and bolstered by the overwhelming reception given their tour group in 1953, the JKA proceeded to prepare instructors for the establishment of their American branch.

In May 1961, Teruyuki Okazaki, revered by many as perhaps the best technical karate man ever born, arrived in Philadelphia as the first official JKA instructor in the U.S. But for all their zeal and expertise, the JKA people encountered difficulties they had not expected in attempting to transplant karate-do in America.

Yoshiaki Ajari

Fumio Demura, left, with Donn Draeger

In what Okazaki later described as "naive judgment," the JKA headquarters allowed him six months to establish his organization and return to Japan. The problem with this plan was that Okazaki did not speak a word of English.

"It was terrible," he recalls. "Mr. Sugiura, a nidan (second degree black belt) from Keio University, helped me as an interpreter when he could, but he was busy most of the time. So, when I went to a restaurant, I would look up and down the menu as if I could read it. When the waitress would come by, I would silently point to an item on the menu. Sometimes it turned out to be steak, and sometimes only soup. After one too many bowls of soup, arrangements were made for me to borrow a menu. Then, at night in my apartment, I would pour over the menu with an English-Japanese dictionary in hand, trying to figure out what each item was."

The language barrier was a problem that was to last for Okazaki for over three years. With tongue in cheek, Okazaki shrugs, "I told the JKA that it was impossible to accomplish much of anything in just six months, so they extended my assignment 'for a while.' That was over forty years ago."

The difficulty in ordering meals was no different for Okazaki than it was for many other immigrants, but his problem was compounded by the fact that he was charged with explaining and teaching a difficult and complex art to people with whom he could not communicate.

"In the early days," he says, "I didn't know how to answer students' questions, because I couldn't understand them. One of the students I could understand told me that I was the sensei, and that students should just shut up and do what I told them to do. So, I just started answering questions with 'Shut up! Just do it!' I used that phrase all the time until I realized that all the students were quitting. Luckily for me, my American wife came along just in time. She explained to me that such a phrase was impolite, and she taught me how to communicate. I just didn't know anything."

From those difficult beginnings, Okazaki oversaw the develop-

Karate Comes to the United States

ment of his East Coast Karate Association into one of the largest and most affluent karate organizations in the United States, first in affiliation with Hidetaka Nishiyama's American Amateur Karate Federation (AAKF), and later independently as the International Shotokan Karate Federation (ISKF). How Okazaki developed his small club in Philadelphia into an international organization with affiliates in the U.S., Canada, Mexico, Central America, South America, and the West Indies will be discussed in the next chapter.

Following Okazaki's lead, other karate men began arriving in the United States at a rapid rate.

In the summer of 1961, Hidetaka Nishiyama returned to the United States to oversee the building of the new empire in North America. From his Los Angeles headquarters, he directed the assignments of some of the most technically proficient karate men to be found anywhere. Takayuki Mikami, twice All Japan Champion, went first to Kansas City and later to New Orleans. Yutaka Yaguchi assisted in Los Angeles for 10 years, and then moved on to develop the organization in Denver.

Hirokazu Kanazawa, also twice All Japan Champion, brought the JKA to Hawaii and was replaced after two years by Masataka Mori, who ultimately went to New York. In Hawaii, he was followed, in succession, by Tetsuhiko Asai and Takehiko Nozaki.

Shojiro Sugiyama, not a graduate of the instructor program, but nevertheless a

Hidetaka Nishiyama (left) shortly after his arrival in the U.S., spars with Takayuki Mikami. In the background, Teruyuki Okazaki (right) spars with Masataka Mori.

respected karate man, founded a strong organization in Chicago. Over the years he has written several popular books on karate and coached the Northwestern University Karate Club to collegiate championships in 1977 and 1984. Among his well-known students are Igor Miletic, 1970 National Champion in free sparring; Ted Hedlund, 4th place in the World Championships in 1975 in free sparring; and Joe Gonzalez, 1984 National Champion.

Tetsuhiko Asai

The list of placements in the 1960s and 1970s is long and impressive: Masaaki Ueki and Shigeru Takashina in Florida, Katsuya Kisaka in New Jersey, Shojiro Koyama in Arizona.

By the mid-1970s, the evangelizing was paying off with a bounty of brilliant American karate instructors, most of whom by this time had 15 or more years of training under the Japanese. The most senior of these was Robert Fusaro of Minneapolis. Fusaro's

Shojiro Sugiyama (front row, center) at a 1965 tournament with some of his first U.S. students.

Karate Comes to the United States

Hiroshi Shirai (left) and Keinosuke Enoeda demonstrate before a large crowd in Chicago during their historic 1965 "All Japan Champions World Tour."

Shojiro Koyama

organization is today one of the largest and strongest in the country.

Other notable instructors in the 1970s included Robert Graves of Oregon; Greer Golden of Ohio; Ray Dalke, Frank Smith, James Yabe, and James Field of California; and Robin Reilly, Leslie Safar, Ronald Johnson, Gerald Evans, and Maynard Miner of the East Coast.

Nishiyama's organization, the All America Karate Federation (now the

Shotokan Karate: Its History and Evolution

Robert Fusaro in a masterful example of tobi-geri

American Amateur Karate Federation), AAKF, finally officially opened its doors to non-JKA karate people in the late 1960s, but it was too little, too late to salvage the original dream of a truly unified American karate under the guidance of the JKA.

This is not to say that Nishiyama did not make a very strong bid to control karate in the United States. Indeed, after opening the doors of the AAKF to non-JKA people, he applied for allied voting

Robert Fusaro (L) and Robert Graves

Karate Comes to the United States

Ray Dalke (Right) with his top student and successor as AJKA Chief Instructor, Edmond Otis.

membership for his organization in the Amateur Athletic Union of the United States (AAU). In his application of November 28, 1970, he claimed "… enrollment of over 20,000 AAKF members in more than 300 U.S. Karate clubs." In addition to 141 individual AAKF karate clubs, Nishiyama's application to the AAU listed Armed Forces Karate Association clubs in California, Washington, Georgia, Michigan, and New Mexico and overseas in Japan, Germany, Guam, and Okinawa. Further, the application listed 50 chapters of the AAKF's Collegiate Karate Union of the U.S. in 24 states, and made the strong point that the AAKF, by virtue of its affiliation with the JKA, was directly tied to an additional 234 JKA clubs in 17 nations, excluding the United States.

The legendary Frank Smith, right, in action against Tonny Tulleners

All America Karate Champion James Yabe competes in the seventh JKA All Japan Karate Championship in Tokyo, 1964.

So strong was Nishiyama's numerical and political clout, that he was able to issue the following news release on November 6, 1971:

> "The Amateur Athletic Union of the United States has been investigating the karate field for the past several years in search of a representative organization for karate in the United States. At the convention held on October 9, at Lake Placid, New York, the All America Karate Federation ... was officially accepted as an allied member for the Amateur Athletic Union of the United States. The Amateur Athletic Union further recognizes the All America Karate Federation as the official representative of karate from the United States.
>
> "John B. Kelly, President of the Amateur

Karate Comes to the United States

Masatoshi Nakayama demonstrates defense against multiple attackers at the First World Invitational Karate-do Championship in Mexico City, on November 4, 1968. On the right is Keinosuke Enoeda. Punching is Nobuhiro Yatoh, and visible to the rear of Nakayama is Hiroshi Matsuura, JKA Chief Instructor for Mexico.

Hidetaka Nishiyama (bottom right) greets the Japanese national team upon its arrival in Los Angeles in 1968 for the First World Invitational Karate-do Tournament. Ehichi Eriguchi of WUKO (left) shakes hands with Gene Takahashi, U.S. Team Representative. Directly behind Takahashi is Kimio Itoh of the JKA, and directly behind Eriguchi is Manzo Iwata of Shito-ryu.

Hidetaka Nishiyama's U.S. Team, considered by many to be the strongest American karate team ever assembled, prepares to depart for Japan in 1967, enroute to the second U.S.-Japan Collegiate Tournament in Tokyo. L-R: Rei Fujikawa, George Takahashi (Chief Secretary, AAKF), Constantine Equinoa, Yutaka Yaguchi (Chief Instructor, AAKF Western Region), Philip Auerbach, Gene Takahashi (Team Coach), Frank Smith, Paul White, Ray Dalke, and Hidetaka Nishiyama.

Athletic Union, stated: 'We are very pleased to accept karate into the Amateur Athletic Union.

"'I think karate has great potential as a sport in the United States. I have seen many tournaments in which high technical proficiency was demonstrated in coordination with maximum control. The excellent training and instruction is evidenced by the lack of serious injuries. The existence of quality karate has determined our decision to accept the All America Karate Federation as an allied member of the Amateur Athletic Union.

Karate Comes to the United States

"'I feel confident that the All America Karate Federation's objectives are to recognize and admit all legitimate karate groups into the organization. It is then this organization's responsibility to form the United States Team for the Second World Championship in Paris, France.

"'It will be quite difficult for karate to be admitted to the Olympics because their program is overcrowded now. However, karate should aim for the 1976 Olympics in Montreal, Canada.'

"The All America Karate Federation, a national organization which includes the Collegiate Karate Union and the Armed Forces Karate Association, has been in existence for 10 years. It has a national membership totaling over 20,000 members.

"Until the present, many karate organizations in the United States were either on a professional or commercial basis; therefore, it was never clear which organization could represent the United States on an amateur basis.

"The events that have taken place on the international scene showed an urgent need for a representative organization in karate for the United States. The First World Karate Championship Tournament was held in 1970. This led to the formation of the only world karate organization, the World Union of Karate-do Organizations. The Second Word Championship Tournament is to be held in April, 1972 in Paris, France.

"The past international activities of the All America Karate Federation, which include the First US-Japan Goodwill Karate Match in 1965, and the 1968 Olympic Commemoration International Invitational Karate Tournament, has brought the

United States recognition as a strong karate power, possibly equaling Japan. Now that the All America Karate Federation has become an Amateur Athletic Union member, it is expected to continue and advance activities in international karate.

"The Chairman of the All America Karate Federation, Hidetaka Nishiyama, said, 'We are very pleased to have karate admitted officially into the Amateur Athletic Union as a sport. The All America Karate Federation will demonstrate the pride and responsibility it has as a representative of the United States. At the same time, as an organization of all amateur karate, we will strive further for its development.'"

While the acceptance of the AAKF by the AAU was the fulfillment of Hidetaka Nishiyama's major domestic goal, it was also due largely to the efforts of a single AAKF administrator, selected because of his many years of work in AAU swimming, A. R. "Dick" Allen.

A. R. Allen, an insurance man with a highly successful business career, joined the AAKF karate club in Portland, Oregon, in the 1960s, on the advice of his physician. Allen suffered from a serious back problem, and the doctor thought that karate, with its emphasis on correct posture and body mechanics, might be helpful. When Allen's instructor, Robert Graves, mentioned to Hidetaka Nishiyama that he had a student who was highly respected in the AAU, the wheels were set in motion for the AAKF to become an AAU member.

Calling upon his vast knowledge of the inner workings of the AAU and collecting on some owed favors from various national administrators, Allen almost single-handedly guided the AAKF in its quest for AAU membership. In fact, it was A. R. Allen who signed the AAKF's application for AAU membership for Hidetaka Nishiyama.

Karate Comes to the United States

With the well-deserved respect of his peers, Allen was elected as the first Chairman of the AAU Karate Committee, and it was largely due to his singular tenacity, business acumen, and political clout that the AAKF was accepted by the AAU.

But even with such brilliant administrators as A. R. Allen behind him, Hidetaka Nishiyama had waited too long to make his move. The rest of the karate community in the U. S. felt scorned by him for many years, and they were not willing to jump on his bandwagon. The overwhelming sentiment among non–AAKF martial artists was that Nishiyama could not be trusted, that he was merely a puppet of the JKA. Nishiyama's first open letter, dated February 5, 1972, to the directors of all karate organizations and clubs in the U.S. did little to assuage their fears:

A. R. Allen

Richard Kim, left, and A. R. Allen

"Gentlemen:

"The recent action of the AAU in recognizing karate as an established international sport is a significant victory for us all. It means, among other things, that karate has emerged from the period of misunderstanding, suspicion, and sensationalism into the bright light of full public acceptance. This is a goal to which we have all been dedicated and we share the victory that has been achieved.

"Since the All America Karate Federation has been designated a voting allied member of the AAU, a certain responsibility falls upon us to see that all legitimate styles of karate are given proper recognition and an opportunity to participate on an equal basis in forthcoming tournament activities. To avoid misunderstandings and to forestall the kind of friction which would be out of place in sportsmanlike competition, I would like to clarify certain points of mutual interest.

"1. It is our position that the further development of the art and sport of karate will be served best by the effective unification of all legitimate karate groups despite differences in individual styles and techniques.

"2. In view of the AAU action in selecting the AAKF as a voting allied member, the AAKF has voluntarily broadened its base so that it can serve as a structural organization incorporating all of the established styles of karate now practiced in the United States.

"3. Henceforth any amateur karate man qualified to join the AAU is both invited and encouraged to participate in AAKF open tournaments. AAKF membership will not be a requirement, furthermore the panel of judges will be made up from the qualified personnel of many different groups if they are available.

"4. All contestants, regardless of affiliation, will be qualified for competition through a basic test designed solely to maintain safety standards through demonstrated control of technique. This qualification, which is common to a great many organized sports, hopefully will prevent fatalities or serious injuries in future competition. All recipients of this letter will be aware that such incidents have occurred in the past; forestalling any in the future is an objective to which we can all subscribe without reservation.

"5. During the elimination tournaments the objective will be to select the best team possible to represent the United States at the forthcoming Second World Karate-do Championship Tournament to be held in Paris this year. To this end full representation by all amateur karate-men qualified for this level of competition is invited and urged.

"At this time I would like to solicit your help and support toward the attainment of these objectives. If you wish further information, or have any questions concerning points not covered in this letter, please contact [the AAKF].

"Very sincerely yours,
"Hidetaka Nishiyama,
Chairman, AAKF"

After one look at this letter, the non-JKA, non-AAKF karate practitioners felt their worst fears had been realized. After all, they reasoned, they had for years borne the brunt of Nishiyama's attacks on their "misunderstanding," "suspicion," and "sensationalism." The fact that Nishiyama's followers had always claimed that most non-JKA styles were not legitimate styles, hardly gave them comfort in hearing that Nishiyama would accept "legitimate" styles and "established" styles. His repeated references to people "qualified to join" and "qualified personnel" gave them little solace either.

As they saw it, Nishiyama was now in a position to officially designate them as unqualified, illegitimate, and unable to pass his "basic test" for control.

Without hesitation, many non-AAKF karate men frantically began organizing themselves into loose coalitions, combining their numbers, and applying for the same status in the AAU as held by the AAKF.

As early as November 24, 1972, Hidetaka Nishiyama was acknowledging their actions and fighting against them. In a letter on that date to John Brooks, Chairman of the AAU Membership Committee, and distributed publicly, Nishiyama wrote:

> "The AAKF is firmly adverse to the acceptance of other allied karate organizations into the AAU. The reasons are as follows:
>
> "1. Under already accepted international karate standards, acceptance of additional technical governing bodies would only add trouble and confusion to present stability.
>
> "Acceptance of additional members, merely upon their request, would bring about unlimited governing bodies representing numerous standards. The present allied member, AAKF, is open to any qualified individuals or clubs with equal rights for all.
>
> "Other karate organizations agree with our international standards but they seem hesitant to enter our 'open doors.' The crux of the problem appears to be emotional or based upon the wish to utilize the AAU name for their own benefit. It is assumed that such personal priorities are not rep-

resentative of AAU tradition.

"2. A single definition of karate and its standardized rules are accepted on a 90% worldwide basis and 100% within World Union of Karate-do Organizations. In the U.S., should an independently oriented allied member be accepted by AAU, friction and unrest within the AAU and between the international bodies are most likely.

"We would sincerely appreciate your considerations of the points mentioned above. If you have any questions or ambiguities, I would be happy to help clear them up."

Perhaps as much to avoid the many conflicts facing them as in response to Hidetaka Nishiyama's reasoning, the AAU administrators chose to reject further applications from karate organizations seeking equal status with the AAKF. But their hopes to avoid conflict were quickly dashed.

In a series of intrigues and political battles rivaling the makings of a first-class adventure novel, the AAU and AAKF severed their ties with each other. In large measure, this was due to political infighting by Nishiyama at the international level, and partly due to incredibly inept administration by the AAU in the U.S.

By 1974, it was all over, and Hidetaka Nishiyama distributed the following news release on May 1, 1975, trying to cut his losses on the domestic scene, and offering justifications for the muddled international situation:

THE AAU AND UNITED STATES KARATE
"In 1971, the All America Karate Federation (AAKF) and the Amateur Athletic Union (AAU) reached an agreement which resulted in the AAKF becoming an allied body of the AAU. The underlying basis for this agreement was that the AAKF and the AAU formally recognized one another.

"In October, 1972, the 2nd World Karate Championship Tournament was held in Paris. The AAKF organized the national trials for the tournament and took the responsibility of sending a team and officials to Paris.

"At the Paris Conference, the AAKF was chosen as the Representative of Amateur Karate in the U.S. However, as a result of political maneuvering by representatives of the AAU, the minutes were changed at a later date to recognize the AAU rather than the AAKF as the representative of United States karate. At the same time, the AAU severed its alliance with the AAKF, despite the fact that according to the articles of alliance between the two organizations advance notice of one year was a prerequisite to cancellation. Immediately thereafter in November of 1972, the AAU announced that it was the international representative of American karate.

"Although the AAU formally severed its relationship with the AAKF, the majority of the AAU Karate Committee members were also members of the AAKF. Therefore, when the AAU held its first karate organizational elections, Mr. A. R. Allen, a member of the AAKF, was elected AAU National Karate Chairman. Mr. Allen had been one of the AAKF delegates to the Paris Conference, where he had strongly opposed the AAU's usurpation of the AAKF's authority.

"The AAU officials were, of course, unhappy that its members had elected Mr. Allen. Consequently, Mr. Allen was ousted from his elected position by the simple device of falsely announcing his resignation. Thereupon the AAU officials replaced Mr. Allen with a person of their choosing.

"The AAU has also had serious differences with the National Collegiate Athletic Association (NCAA). More than half of the AAKF members belong to collegiate clubs, but karate is not yet a sport of the NCAA, although the relationship between AAKF and NCAA is very good. Nevertheless, AAKF has maintained a neutral position visávis the AAU and NCAA.

"... transitional forces are now affecting international sports as well. The 1975 World Karate-do Championship Tournament is a good case in point. In September of 1974 WUKO (World Union of Karate-do Organizations) held a special meeting in New York at which the IAKF (International

The first IAKF conference in Los Angeles in August, 1975. A. R. Allen is at the podium.

Amateur Karate Federation) was officially established. The AAKF was recognized as the representative of the United States and was also assigned as host of the upcoming World Karate-do Championship. However, the organizations of several countries

(Left to right): Teruyuki Okazaki, A. R. Allen, and Eiichi Eriguchi, head of WUKO in the 1970s

which opposed the democratic meeting held in New York have used the WUKO name in planning their own 'world championship', scheduled to be held in Long Beach, California, under the auspices of the AAU and directed by Mr. Ed Parker. This event has no connections whatsoever with our own championship to be presented by the IAKF.

THE INTERNATIONAL AMATEUR KARATE FEDERATION: A BRIEF HISTORY

"Since 1970, the world karate population has

Karate Comes to the United States

worked tirelessly to establish an international karate organization. Much of this work was conducted under the name of the World Union of Karate-do Organizations (WUKO). In spite of their efforts, unfortunate circumstances arose over the years which caused many setbacks in their progress. But finally, in 1974 the International Amateur Karate Federation (IAKF) was established. What follows is a brief history of that organization.

"In both the First World Karate Championship (Tokyo, 1970) and the Second World Championship (Paris, 1972), the tournament hosts were allowed to select the participants without reference to any set qualifications or standard. As a result, many national karate organizations, the European ones in particular, were denied equal tournament participation.

"As a result, many countries were deeply disap-

The U.S. contingent to the WUKO World Championships in front of their hotel in Paris, France, in 1972. In front is John Gehlsen. Far left is Leslie Safar. To Gehlsen's rear (left) is George Byrd, and behind him is Teruyuki Okazaki. Behind Gehlsen (right) is Frank Smith, and behind him is Tonny Tulleners. Far right is James Yabe, and behind him is Richard Kim.

pointed in WUKO, the sponsor, and there was a general feeling that the tournament itself was not a success.

"Although preparations for the international federation had begun in 1970, two conferences had been held only (in a four year period) and no decision had been reached on either a basic organizational constitution, or simple rules and regulations.

"At the Paris conference, officers were selected but still no real administrational rules were decided upon. Karate people began to recognize WUKO as a fraudulent organization for the private use of a few people. The administration had always been conducted in a dictator-like style by the championship hosts and small groups from France and parts of Japan.

"Confusions abounded, factionalism grew rampant as a result, the designated hosts for the next World Championship Tournament were forced to stop all preparations and WUKO itself came to a standstill.

"The world karate organizations recommended that a World Conference be arranged to return WUKO to stable conditions.

"Mr. A. R. Allen, WUKO vice-president and tournament host representative, called a Third World Championship Preparation Conference in verbal agreement with WUKO Headquarters. A meeting notice was sent to all known national karate organizations and the cooperation was asked of all national Olympic committees.

"Prior to the meeting, a group of WUKO officers tried to prevent the meeting by sending telegrams to the various organizations stating that the meeting was not recognized by WUKO on the

Karate Comes to the United States

basis that it did not follow the WUKO rules. The telegram was meaningless as WUKO itself had established no rules for anyone to follow. The special meeting was held as planned on September 27, 1974, in New York City with the representatives of 25 countries in attendance.

"The New York Conference marked great achievements as it was the first time that a conference had been arranged by majority request, the first time that all countries had been informed of the meeting, and, also, the first time that everyone had been extended an equal participation opportunity since the beginnings of the WUKO structure.

"An appeal was sent to the WUKO president, asking him to respect the decisions of the Paris Conference. In addition, the appeal asked that the system of participant selection by the host for the World Championships be replaced by a common and democratic standard for participation, one which would allow everyone an equal opportunity for participation.

"At the meeting it was decided that: In the event the appeal was denied or ignored, all decisions of the New York Conference would be effective automatically; the AAKF was to be reinstated as host of the Third World Championship to be held in Los Angeles, California, in 1975; and, an international karate organization, one which would be so necessary to the smooth running operations of the championship, would be established. WUKO, the preparatory formation organization would change its name to the IAKF, an IAKF constitution was adopted, and officers, whose terms lasted until the Third World Championship, were elected according to the constitution.

"Unlike past WUKO Conferences, the New York Conference typified a voluntary assembly with an equality of participation and representation. Because the constitution had been adopted, all decisions were made constitutionally.

"The appeal to WUKO President was denied, and the IAKF was officially established on September 27, 1974 as the international karate organization. The AAKF was also renamed as championship host and resumed preparations according to the decisions of the New York Conference.

"The Pan American Karate Union, which is composed of 15 Western Hemisphere countries, officially recognized the IAKF at their conference. By February, 1975, 44 countries had recognized the actions taken at the New York Conference.

"At the next IAKF conference, all national karate organizations will have an equal opportunity to participate. All rules and regulations shall be discussed openly, officers shall be elected by a written constitution, and all matters of concern to an international sports organization shall be presented.

"The IAKF holds the principles of equality of participation in high esteem. The administration is run democratically and openly, with stated rules and regulations. The IAKF is now initiating procedures which will establish it as an official international sports organization."

No sooner had the AAKF put to rest the difficult problem of the AAU than an internal upheaval split its ranks and severely limited Nishiyama's power in the United States. As will be seen later, all the years of frustration and confusion took their toll on the

Karate Comes to the United States

membership as well as the instructors, ultimately culminating in the resignation of Teruyuki Okazaki and the formation of the International Shotokan Karate Federation (ISKF), another JKA affiliate in the U.S.

Until its splintering after the death of Masatoshi Nakayama in 1987, the Japan Karate Association was the largest and most unified organization of its kind in the world.

Taiji Kase, the most senior instructor in Europe, made his headquarters in Paris, France. Of the 32 official JKA instructors on assignment outside of Japan, eight were located in the United States—Hidetaka Nishiyama, Teruyuki Okazaki, Takayuki Mikami, Masataka Mori, Yutaka Yaguchi, Katsuya Kisaka, Shojiro Koyama, and Shigeru Takashina. Other official instructors on assignment included Yoshiaki Habu in Malaysia, Kunio Sasaki in the Philippines, Hideki Okamoto in Egypt, Mitsuo Inouye in Argentina, Satoshi Miyazaki in Belgium, Yasuyuki Fujinaga in Austria, Hideo Ochi in West Germany, Hiroshi Shirai and Takeshi Naito in Italy, Keinosuke Enoeda and Masao Kawazoe in Great Britain, Osamu Aoki in Spain, Hidetoshi Ebata and Minako Kondo in Abudhabi, Koichi Sugimura in Switzerland, and Tetsuo Odake in Greece. On equal ground with the United States in the number of official JKA instructors assigned there was Brazil with Sadaru Uriu, Tetsuma Higashino, Yasuyuki Sasaki, Taketo Okuda, Yasutaka Tanaka, Juichi Sagara, and Yoshizo Machida.

The most noteworthy and famous non-Japanese JKA instruc-

Taiji Kase

Shotokan Karate: Its History and Evolution

Taiji Kase, left, spars with Keinosuke Enoeda in the 1960s.

tor outside the United States is Stan Schmidt of South Africa. Schmidt was the first non-Japanese *shichi-dan* (seventh degree black belt) of the JKA, and he oversees a huge South African organization, while occasionally starring in and/or directing the fighting choreography for internationally distributed motion pictures.

Thus it is that JKA Shotokan karate-do is now practiced daily by more than five million people in almost every country in the world.

While the JKA has led the way in internationalizing karate, this is not to imply that there is not a large contingent of people practicing Gichin Funakoshi's karate outside the auspices of the JKA. Several of Funakoshi's best pupils chose to leave the Shotokan structure altogether and develop their own, eclectic systems, which still bear similitude to Funakoshi's karate-do. Notable among these are Yasuhiro Konishi, who founded the Shindo-Jinen-ryu (commonly known as Ryobukan), and Hironori Ohtsuka, who developed the Wado-ryu.

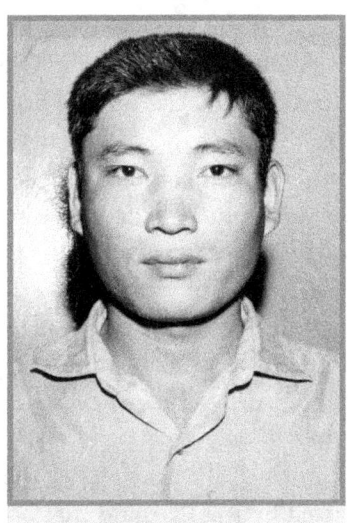

Kunio Sasaki

Karate Comes to the United States

Hiroshi Shirai

Stan Schmidt, right, of South Africa

But the key Shotokan karate in Japan, outside the JKA, remains connected to the Old Boys in the universities. Following Isao Obata, head of the Old Boys at Keio University, in his early exodus from the JKA were Genshin Hironishi of Chuo University, and Hiroshi Noguchi and Shigeru Egami of Waseda University. It was from Waseda University that Tsutomu Ohshima came to the United States in 1956 and ultimately founded Shotokan Karate of America.

Today, the most popular Shotokan karate in Japan outside the JKA is probably Shotokan Karate International, which was founded by Hirokazu Kanazawa after his break with the JKA in the 1970s.

Until the mid-1970s, the differences between the karate practiced by the JKA and that of other Shotokan groups were slight. In 1976, however, Shigeru Egami published a book titled *The Way of Karate, Beyond Technique*. In it, Tsutomu Ohshima, a popular fig-

Stan Schmidt, left, receives his sandan (third degree black belt) diploma on national television in Japan

ure in the United States and Europe, introduced Egami as the inheritor of Gichin Funakoshi's position as leader of the karate world. Just prior to the release of this book, Genshin Hironishi, another of Funakoshi's original students, arranged for the publication in English of several newspaper essays written by Funakoshi in 1956. Collecting these together, Hironishi purported them to be the autobiography of the master, and he proclaimed that he, Hironishi, was President of an organization called the Japan Karate-do Shoto-kai. While in reality the Shoto-kai, or "Shoto's Association," that Hironishi speaks of is a very small group of people in Japan composed mainly of the Old Boys at Waseda University, the book served to promote the image of the organization in the United States. It seems clear that Hironishi's intentions were completely honorable in presenting the so-called "autobiography" of his master, but the book, along with Egami's efforts the following year, served to foster the false impression of a large, powerful organization officially designated by Gichin Funakoshi to pass his art on to future generations.

The fact of the matter is that the only organization ever officially, publicly, and actively sanctioned by Gichin Funakoshi was the Japan Karate Association. According to Teruyuki Okazaki, Funakoshi was present and active at the JKA headquarters dojo virtually every day until the week before his death.

When Egami's book appeared, it described techniques and training methods that were never part of Gichin Funakoshi's karate-do. Using photos of early Japanese masters, Egami pointed to these photos as the wrong way to perform techniques, and he proposed that karate be changed completely.

Among other things, he changed the form of the fist, the most basic technique of Gichin Funakoshi's karate, insisting that the wrist always be bent, and that the middle knuckle always be extended. He further decried the use of the makiwara as a training device, and implied that meditation would lead the practitioner to the truth of karate-do better than would rigorous training.

For his part, Tsutomu Ohshima published a translation of Karate-do Kyohan in English in 1973, for the most part presenting the techniques as they were originally practiced by Gichin Funakoshi. His subsequent approval of Egami's efforts has since caused confusion in a few minds. Apparently, Ohshima, one of the most popular forces in Shotokan karate in the U.S. outside of the JKA, is following the technical path prescribed by Egami, a path which is distinctly different from Gichin Funakoshi's original karate.

Another important and noticeable difference between the JKA and the Shoto-kai groups at Waseda and in the United States is that the latter practice Taikyoku and Ten-no-kata, training forms created by Genshin Hironishi and Giko Funakoshi, but which were never taught by Gichin Funakoshi to anyone at the Japan Karate Association. Masatoshi Nakayama was emphatic on this point:

> "Master Funakoshi never taught us those forms. They were created as basic training methods by Yoshitaka (Giko) Funakoshi and Genshin Hironishi, but they were never taught or practiced by Master Funakoshi. The principles of these forms do not conform to the principles of *kata*. They are not *kata;* they are basic training methods. But they were never taught by Master Funakoshi.
>
> "Master Minoru Miyata was asked by Yoshitaka Sensei and Genshin Hironishi to pose for photographs to illustrate the movements of

Taikyoku and Ten-no-kata, and out of respect for Yoshitaka, the Master's son, he consented. But even though the photos of Mr. Miyata were used to introduce these forms, he, himself, never learned them or practiced them. In Japan, the only group that knows these forms is the Waseda University group. Even Keio University, the oldest of the Shotokan clubs, has no knowledge of them.

"...Both before and after my trip to China (1937-1946), I trained with Master Funakoshi virtually every day, and he never once mentioned Taikyoku or Ten-no-kata. Not even once.

"...I can tell you that they positively are not in the original Japanese version (of *Karate-do Kyohan*)."2

Critics of Nakayama pointed out for years that the kata do appear in the 1958 edition of Karate-do Kyohan, but Nakayama in turn replied that the 1958 edition was published after Fuanakoshi's death and could easily have been changed without his knowledge.

Finally, in an interview published in the September 1987 issue of *Black Belt* magazine, Tsutomu Ohshima, the man who translated the 1958 edition of Karate-do Kyohan into English, was questioned directly about the matter by Jim Rosenthal, assistant editor of *Black Belt:*

"BB (Rosenthal): Are the 19 forms published in Funakoshi's book the basis for your Shotokan karate?"

OHSHIMA: Not exactly. Master Funakoshi never really taught the ten-no kata *(kata* of the heaven) or the three taikyoku (first cause) forms. When he got to Tokyo from Okinawa in the early 20th century, Master Funakoshi was pressed to

Karate Comes to the United States

reveal how many *kata* he knew. If he said he knew 20, someone else would say they know 50. The same thing happened to me when I got to the United States. People ask how many *kata* you know, and the more you say the more they think of you. That is ridiculous. Master Funakoshi said that to practice *kata* is not to memorize an order—even the 15 kata are too much. You must find the *kata* that work for you, understand them, digest them, and stick with them for life. That is a very honest approach. Life is too short to understand everything. Master Funakoshi didn't want us to just load up on learning many *kata*. The principle behind the *kata* is the most important thing. We must keep trying to teach a higher level of mentality."[3]

Tsutomu Ohshima

Another major difference between the Shotokan factions is that from about 1955 forward, the JKA has strongly pursued the study of karate from the viewpoint of scientific analysis of body mechanics, kinesiology, anatomy, physics, and modern psychology. This, contend most of the Shoto-kai people, is unnecessary and detrimental to the traditional ways taught by Funakoshi.

During his last years, Funakoshi frequently taught at the Yotsuya dojo of the JKA, tirelessly teaching the deeper meanings of the art to the protégés who he knew would have to pass it along to future generations.

6
The JKA in the United States

Even the most noble and philanthropic organizations experience internal strife from time to time, and the Japan Karate Association has not been exempted from its share of political problems.

To understand what has happened to the JKA in the United States, it is important first to understand the image created in the minds of Americans by the JKA Japanese instructors, themselves.

As noted earlier, there were a few Americans teaching various styles of karate in the U.S. in 1961, but not one of them possessed the expertise of the JKA instructors who were dispatched from the JKA headquarters in Tokyo. In most cases, the American karate men had learned their skills in the service, while stationed in Asia, and it was unusual to find one with more than two to four years of total karate experience.

The JKA men, on the other hand, had been training steadily since the 1940s, and many of them had completed the most rigorous instructor training program imaginable. These were men with 15 or more years of almost fulltime training, whose whole lives were devoted to karate, and the difference between the strength and precision of their techniques and those of their American

A 1967 meeting in Minneapolis, Minnesota, of JKA leaders. Left to right: Teruyuki Okazaki, Robert Fusaro, Hidetaka Nishiyama, Shojiro Sugiyama

counterparts was stunning—particularly to the Americans.

For a short time after their arrival, the JKA men were courted by the Americans who had studied karate in Asia. They were revered and sought after, their skills elevated in the minds of the Americans to almost mystical proportions. American instructors flocked to them with hopes of learning and with hopes of being accepted by them as karate masters. But the JKA men had been raised in such a rigid hierarchical structure in Japan, that they saw no reason to grant any quarter to the Americans.

Two of the better-known American instructors of the time—one of them claiming to be a seventh degree black belt, and the other a fifth degree—enrolled in the dojo of one of the JKA masters in 1961. They were told that their ranking would not be recognized, but that they would be given an evaluation examination after an appropriate period of training. Secure in their belief that their rankings would be recognized, the two men began training

The first Missouri Karate Championship Tournament in St. Louis, Missouri, in April, 1968. Left to right: Judges Robert Fusaro, Shojiro Sugiyama, Takayuki Mikami, Teruyuki Okazaki, Hidetaka Nishiyama, and Tournament Director Randall Hassell

The JKA in the United States

with gusto. When, a short time later, the seventh degree black belt was evaluated at the level of eighth *kyu*, the lowest beginner's ranking, the fifth degree decided to cut his losses, go home, and form his own organization—an organization that competes with the JKA organizations to this day.

The first JKA black belt examination held in the U.S. in 1961. The board of examiners, from left to right, Toshio Sugiura, Hirokazu Kanazawa, Hidetaka Nishiyama, and Teruyuki Okazaki.

Whether or not the examination was conducted fairly is not the subject of scrutiny here. The simple fact that the examination results were so far away from the Americans' perceptions of their own skills is exemplary of why the JKA instructors immediately fell from grace with the Americans.

This incident and many more similar ones set the tone for the relationship between the JKA instructors and non-JKA American karate practitioners. The JKA men felt that the Americans didn't know anything about karate and, therefore, should follow the JKA way. The Americans, on the other hand, felt that the JKA instructors, while obviously superior in skill, knowledge, and experience, were egotistical in the extreme. In some quarters, the messy situation was viewed as racist by both sides, and in many ways, it still is today.

Nevertheless, the JKA instructors continued to arrive in the U.S., and they scattered themselves geographically, each setting up his own independent organization, but still owing allegiance to the headquarters, run by Hidetaka Nishiyama in Los Angeles.

From 1961 to the present day, the JKA in America has set itself apart from all other karate organizations, and while signifi-

Action from the first Missouri Karate Championship Tournament in St. Louis, Missouri, in April, 1968. Takayuki Mikami is the referee. Seated behind him are Randall Hassell, Tournament Director, and Hidetaka Nishiyama, Chief Judge.

cant gains have been made in numbers, the organization has never been able to overcome its image of aloofness in the minds of people in other organizations.

While the other organizations were fighting against the JKA and AAKF, they could not have known that the true seeds of destruction and dissent lay within the organization itself.

Following the debacle of the AAKF's association with the AAU and its incessant focus on international, rather than domestic matters, things began unraveling from the inside out.

By 1975, the glue that had bound the JKA men together for so long (their belief that they alone possessed the best and only true karate in the world) was still intact, but the organization's repeated failures in its attempts to dominate U.S. karate were becoming an

James Yabe, left, faces his teacher, Hidetaka Nishiyama, 1961.

The JKA in the United States

Takayuki Mikami demonstrating at a tournament in 1982

Takayuki Mikami, Yutaka Yaguchi, Shojiro Koyama and Shigeru Takashina) publicly declared the international and national karate scene to be "agitated and con-fusing," and they submitted to the JKA in Tokyo a declaration of opinion entitled, "Suggested Alterations Necessary for Improved Management of Japan Karate Association International of the United

embarrassment. Other organizations were larger, better organized, and generally more attractive to the average person seeking karate instruction. The JKA men felt they were losing face in both domestic and international karate, and they turned their ire toward their U.S. leader, Hidetaka Nishiyama.

On June 12, 1976, the JKA dream of domination of a unified U.S. karate was shattered. On that date, five official JKA representatives in the U.S. (Teruyuki Okazaki,

Teruyuki Okazaki demonstrates his famous roundhouse kick on a tall opponent.

Shigeru Takashina demonstrating at a tournament in 1982

States." Noting that they had asked Mr. Nishiyama to attend a meeting with them, but that his busy schedule would not permit it, they addressed themselves to what they called "Problematic Issues Caused By a Disunity of Activity and Lack of Communication Between Instructors Residing in the United States."

Among other things, they listed the problems as a "self-righteous attitude" in decision-making by Nishiyama, misjudgments of plan and policymaking, a lack of solidarity among JKA instructors in the U.S., an estrangement from reality on the part of Nishiyama, a lack of centralized policymaking, and a lack of planned public relations activities "to influence the growth and cohesion of Japan Karate Association karate in the United States." They asserted that the All America Karate Federation had "continuously and deliberately ignored" their suggestions in all matters of policy, and they called for a general reorganization.

In Japan, their complaints fell on deaf ears, at least officially. The JKA leaders in Japan tried sincerely, but in vain, to get all the instructors to cooperate. Their situation was made more sensitive by the fact that the JKA in Japan had already pledged allegiance to Nishiyama's International Amateur Karate Federation, and a breakup of their American-based instructors would be a devastating public embarrassment.

The JKA in the United States

Nevertheless, in spite of all the negotiations, the five dissenting instructors threw down the gauntlet before Zentaro Kosaka, President of the Japan Karate Association, in a letter dated June 19, 1977. In the letter, they decried the "worsening situation" in JKA karate in America, and predicted its "deterioration and subsequent demise" if their demands were not met. They demanded Nishiyama's resignation for the purpose of "effecting reform and reorganization of Japan Karate Association International of the United States system." If this demand was not met, they warned, they would establish a separate and independent branch of the JKA-US, and would seek JKA recognition for their new organization.

Yutaka Yaguchi (right)

On July 18, 1977, the JKA headquarters forcefully responded to the demands with a document entitled "Request (Demand)." Signed by Masatomo Takagi, Vice-Chairman of the JKA, Masatoshi Nakayama, Chief Instructor, and Kimio Itoh, Chief Secretary, the document flatly stated that while the business practices of Nishiyama's IAKF, AAKF, and Pan American Karate Union appeared to be involved and entangled, the problems the instructors were experiencing were a direct result of lack of communications among themselves. It demanded that each instructor reconsider his original purpose abroad, and "become seriously absorbed in and conscientiously devoted to the existence of Japan Karate Association

Karate-do." It told them to find a concrete method of cooperation to achieve the "singular end" of "spreading Japan Karate Association Karate through (Nishiyama's) organizations."

Within two weeks, the instructors reported to the JKA headquarters that they had met in Los Angeles with Nishiyama on July 30, 1977, and that he had unilaterally rejected all their demands. They said they could not understand Nishiyama's position, and they reiterated their belief that their earlier letter to the JKA was justified.

By September 1, 1977, it was clear to Nishiyama that the instructors were going to break from the organization, and he issued a statement to all JKA-US members, ominously titled, WARNING. In it he noted that some JKA-US instructors were attempting to form what he termed "private karate groups," and he admonished all members to beware of this movement. He explained that anyone who formed or joined such an organization would be automatically expelled from JKA-US and would lose all connections with Japan.

Realizing that they had no choice, the dissenting JKA instructors capitalized on the general dissatisfaction within the JKA-US, and called for a meeting of all the people who had expressed dissatisfaction with the organization. In September, they all tendered their resignations to the AAKF and publicly issued the following declaration:

> RESOLUTION
>
> WHEREAS, we, the representatives of various karate regions of the United States, JKA style, have been asked to convene in order to discuss possible solutions to the numerous administrative problems and inequitable decisions which have afflicted JKA-US over the past ten years; and
>
> WHEREAS, for this purpose, we have assembled in continual sessions at Denver, Colorado, on Saturday and Sunday, September 17 and 18, 1977; and

The JKA in the United States

WHEREAS, it has become apparent (sic) that we share in the common disapproval of the limited perspectives, and repressive policies and decisions which have been demonstrated repeatedly by the hierarchy of JKA-US during the past ten years, as recently exemplified by its unilateral decision to arbitrarily ban a team from participation in the 1977 world tournament, which was held at Tokyo, Japan;

NOW THEREFORE, after open deliberations, we, the representatives of various karate regions in the United States, seeking to protect and to stimulate JKA style karate to more progressive levels, have resolved to create a new national organization. This new organization shall afford open participation to its constituency in the policy and decision making processes.

IT IS FURTHER RESOLVED, that the new national organization shall embrace all JKA style Karate Clubs in the United States; and that, after its formation, an application for its admittance to JKA International, Tokyo, Japan, shall be submitted. In the event that the application is not accepted, the new national organization shall pursue its independent destiny in fostering karate-do, JKA style, in the United States.

In addition to the signatures of the five dissenting JKA instructors, the resolution bore the signatures of 17 American instructors and officials from all over the country.

As correctly anticipated by the dissenting group, Hidetaka Nishiyama was not long in responding. In a public newsletter dated October, 1977, Nishiyama said, "...the JKA-US is not a Japanese instructor's organization, but an organization of American members." He again characterized the new organization as a private interest group acting against the interests of karate-do. He asked for support from American JKA-US members, and said, "We do not need those individuals who lose sight of the real values and goals of karate."

On December 28 of the same year, Nishiyama corresponded with all the JKA member organizations in the Western Hemisphere, this time referring to the organization as the "so-called International Shotokan Karate Federation" and naming Teruyuki Okazaki as the leader. Nishiyama claimed that ISKF had no connections with the JKA in Japan or any of his organizations, and likened the group to Shotokan Karate International, founded by Hirokazu Kanazawa following his expulsion from the JKA in 1977. He said that some individuals cannot make the transition from "family type" groups to world-scale movements. "These by-products of rapid growth fall away from the main body, often for personal interests, and eventually fade from sight," he said, and he asked everyone to keep in mind the common goals of karate as a worldwide union based on
cooperation and unification.

By May 1978, it was clear that Nishiyama was incorrect in his assertion that the dissenters were no longer associated with the JKA in Japan. On May 26, JKA President Zentaro Kosaka informed Teruyuki Okazaki that all the JKA instructors in the U.S. were still recognized as qualified in all respects by the JKA headquarters, but that the JKA recognized only the AAKF as a qualified organization.

For more than a year, negotiations continued between ISKF and Japan until finally, on February 6, 1980, all the concerned parties agreed in writing to operate independently, but to continue to seek cooperation among themselves.

By mid-1980, the seeking of cooperation had been forgotten, and the JKA in Japan quietly began accepting the rankings and qualifications of the ISKF.

By 1981, the ISKF had grown to equal size with the AAKF, and had begun vigorous international expansion. Unfortunately,

The JKA in the United States

this rapid growth soon took its toll on the time and attention of the Japanese instructors.

What began in 1977 as a democratic organization with a full voice for all, as Teruyuki Okazaki characterized it, was, by 1982, beginning to look more and more like a copy of Nishiyama's AAKF.

Many of the promises made in 1977 were not fulfilled, and many of the senior Americans who had pledged their allegiance to Okazaki and ISKF began pushing hard for some action. No matter how many times the subject of instructor and examiner qualifications for Americans was brought up, the answer always came back, "We just have to wait a while for that," or, "We have no control over that; it's up to Japan."

At a special meeting of the ISKF Board of Directors in Denver in 1982, the senior Americans made the point to the Japanese instructors that many fulltime American JKA instructors had been continuously active for more than 15 years, and had not received official instructor or examiner training because it had not been available to them. It was strongly emphasized that these instructors had already produced 3rd and 4th dan students without the aid of the Japanese, and that since they obviously knew what they were doing, they should receive some sort of official qualification.

Again, the answer was the same: "We have no control over that."

By 1983, the senior Americans, led by Ray Dalke of the West Coast, Leslie Safar of the East Coast, Randall Hassell of the Midwest, and A.R. Allen, karate's magnificent elder statesman, decided to act decisively. They presented their views in writing to Teruyuki Okazaki, requesting that their views be aired at the ISKF Board of Directors meeting in November, 1983, in Miami, Florida. The major points they emphasized were:

> 1. It was time for an American administration of karate in the United States, with the Japanese instructors concentrating on providing their tech-

Three of the five founders of the American JKA Karate Association. Left to right, Leslie Safar, Richard Gould, and Ray Dalke

nical expertise, just as karate had developed in virtually every other country on earth.

2. They expressed exasperation with all the previous organizations, i.e., JKA-US, AAKF, ISKF, and expressed a wish for peacefulness along American business and cultural lines.

3. They asked for written (in English), non-capricious rules by which all JKA karate-ka in the U.S. could comport themselves.

4. They said that if Japan was solely responsible for instructor and examiner licenses and the issuance of higher ranking, they would pay to bring JKA Chief Instructor Masatoshi Nakayama, or anyone else the JKA in Japan designated, to the U.S. to specially evaluate them in these areas, and would abide by his decisions.

5. The point was made that they, as the most

The JKA in the United States

senior American JKA karate instructors, had been largely responsible for keeping JKA karate-do alive in the U.S. through their clubs, tournaments, publishing, study, research, and time in grade.

Without responding to these suggestions, Teruyuki Okazaki almost immediately flew from his headquarters in Philadelphia to Los Angeles, where he personally presided over a meeting that resulted in the firing of Ray Dalke as the ISKF West Coast Regional Director. Emphasizing that Dalke had made unkind comments about his Japanese instructors in the press, Okazaki effectively removed Dalke's voice from the Board of Directors.

Ray Dalke (left) referred to by Sports Illustrated as a "brilliant protégé" of Hidetaka Nishiyama, here displays his masterful form and highly respected power, stopping his opponent in mid-charge.

Fearing that the administration of the ISKF was being taken out of their hands, the President and Vice President of ISKF, A. R. Allen and Everett L. King, wrote a letter to Okazaki on September 26, 1983, indicating that they had heard rumors of serious difficulties in Dalke's region.

They said, "It seems to us...that matters of this gravity indicate that some contact with other officials of the organization might be both wise and helpful, and indeed, we respectfully suggest some consultation with us by the administration of the organization before any definitive or substantive decisions are made." They also urged that "...you and the administrators...bring this matter to the attention of the Board of Directors at the National Tournament in November in Miami."

Realizing that their cause was probably lost, the Americans nevertheless decided to make one last stand for their beliefs at the ISKF Board of Directors meeting. After putting their views in writing and carefully considering their position, they appointed A.R. Allen to represent them to the Directors.

Much to everyone's surprise, Allen was summarily removed from his longstanding position of Chairman at the national meeting, and Okazaki took charge. None of the Americans' views were presented to the ISKF Board of Directors.

Feeling discouraged, disillusioned, and betrayed, many of the Americans felt they had no other option but to form a separate organization, just as Okazaki had done several years before.

On November 23, 1984, they issued the following news release to the press and to JKA karate clubs nationwide:

NATIONAL KARATE ORGANIZATION FORMED

Many of the most senior American JKA karate instructors and administrators from all parts of the country gathered on November 21, 1984, to express their views on the state of karate in America, and to lay a foundation for the future growth and development of JKA karate-do in the U.S. by announcing the

The JKA in the United States

formation of the AMERICAN JKA KARATE ASSOCIATIONS (AJKA).

Mr. A. R. Allen, past President of the American Amateur Karate Federation (AAKF), the International Shotokan Karate Federation (ISKF) and the National AAU Karate Committee, was unanimously elected Chairman of the newly formed AJKA.

In a statement issued at the conclusion of the meeting, Chairman Allen described the purpose and goals of the AJKA.

> "Our main purpose," he said, "is to offer an organization of, by, and for American JKA karate and American JKA practitioners. It is our strong feeling that the technical levels and administrative expertise of the senior American JKA karate people have risen to levels which can support and administer the affairs of JKA karate practitioners in this country."
>
> "This does not mean," he continued, "that we are 'jumping ship' and starting over from scratch. Everyone in our organization has great respect and admiration for the Japanese teachers in this country and abroad, and we sincerely do not want to offer the AJKA as an organization in conflict with any other organizations or individuals. As a matter of fact, one of the hallmarks of the AJKA, as clearly spelled out in our Statement of Association, is that we will impose no restrictions whatever on any of our members. They are free to administer their own affairs independently and to work with and cooperate with anyone they choose.
>
> "One of the main purposes of the AJKA, stated in our bylaws, is to '...cooperate with and fully support the aims, purposes, goals and activities of all other JKA-affiliated individuals and groups both domestically and internationally.'

"What is different about the AJKA is that it is structured in a manner which separates the administration of the organization from the technical side. Our Executive Director, Mr. Randall G. Hassell, runs the day-to-day business of the organization, and our Technical Directors, Mr. Ray Dalke and Mr. Leslie Safar, concentrate fully on technical matters. We just don't believe, given the vast number of people involved in JKA karate in this country, that any one person can completely oversee both the technical and administrative sides of an organization. What we are trying to do is free everyone in our organization to utilize their unique skills and talents to the best of their abilities."

Allen explained that the AJKA welcomes the membership of anyone who practices JKA-style karate, and he said that every effort will be made to provide direct affiliation between the AJKA and the Japan Karate Association of Tokyo, Japan.

"When we say 'American JKA'," he explained, "we are simply saying that ours is an American organization which practices the JKA style of karate. We have indeed applied to Japan for affiliation to the Japan Karate Association, because our first love is JKA style karate, and we would prefer to be affiliated with the Tokyo headquarters."

Following a personal meeting with Mr. Masahiko Tanaka, International Director of the Japan Karate Association, Allen presented him with a formal letter of application which read, in part, "...The AJKA, as expressed in the enclosed bylaws, proposes a continued affiliation with the Japan Karate Association International and further proposes to abide by J.K.A. technical qualifications..."

In further describing the aims of the AJKA, Allen's letter

The JKA in the United States

explained, "...We further expect to maintain a direct relationship with JKA International...(and) we propose to maintain a continued friendly relationship with all other JKA instructors and students, not only in the United States, but wherever they may be."

In summation, the application clearly stated, "We have no international aim; we merely wish to maintain our United States independence free from any political interference."

"I have no doubt," Allen said, "that the AJKA will prove to be a valuable and viable organization which will exert a positive influence on the future of karate in America."

The Americans expected to be rejected for membership in the Japan Karate Association, and they expected to be vilified by ISKF organizational newsletters and memoranda, but nothing surprised them more than the manner in which these things occurred.

On December 11, 1984, the AJKA instructors and administrators were informed in a letter from Kimio Itoh, Executive Director of the Japan Karate Association, that not only had their application for membership been rejected, but that they had been summarily stripped of their rankings, instructor, examiner, and judges licenses, and that they would not be admitted to any other organizations affiliated with the JKA.

Even that, however, did not compare with the shock of a letter from Teruyuki Okazaki addressed to all the black belt students of Dalke, Safar, and Hassell.

Dated January 3, 1985, the letter explained that by resigning from the ISKF, the instructors had forfeited their membership, ranking, and qualifications in the Japan Karate Association, and demanded that each black belt formally declare allegiance to ISKF no later than January 28, 1985, or they would suffer the same fate as their instructors. Rather than scare the black belts into renouncing their instructors, however, this letter was generally viewed as a distasteful blacklisting tactic, and it in fact helped provide cohesion among the few black belts who had doubts about the formation of AJKA.

Surprised by what they considered to be unseemly tactics, the AJKA instructors and administrators realized that they would in fact have to act forcefully to protect themselves against what was starting to appear as a campaign of revenge against them. In a lengthy letter to Kimio Itoh on January 16, 1985, the AJKA leaders acknowledged the rejection of their membership application and indicated that they accepted that decision. After specifying their exact reasons for leaving ISKF, they said:

> "...The average length of karate practice of the American members of the ISKF Board of Directors is near 25 years. Because of this, we maintain great respect for our Japanese teachers, and this makes it impossible for us to speak out as boldly against them as we would against administrators who are not great karate masters.
>
> "The point that must be made is that when the voices of dissent are quelled without a fair and impartial hearing, the concept of democracy becomes a fraud. This is true in any organization or state which purports to be democratically organized and administered.
>
> "...as a principle of both law and fairness, it must be acknowledged that honest men of good character can disagree without dishonoring each other or the principles for which each stands.
>
> "...We are adult American citizens who have worked long and hard to earn our qualifications, and we simply cannot stand idly by and watch the work of our lifetimes be eradicated by one stroke of a pen. Such an action would be ethically and morally wrong..."

The JKA in the United States

No response to the letter was ever received, but the furor died quietly. The AJKA withdrew its application for membership in the Japan Karate Association and declared its technical and administrative independence from all other organizations.

The cover story of the May, 1985, issue of Black Belt magazine featured Ray Dalke, and was entitled, "Birth of the American JKA: U.S. Karate Comes of Age." Following publication of this story, the AJKA grew very rapidly, and yet another evolutionary step was taken in the long, complex, and perplexing history of Shotokan karate-do.

7
Ideal and Reality

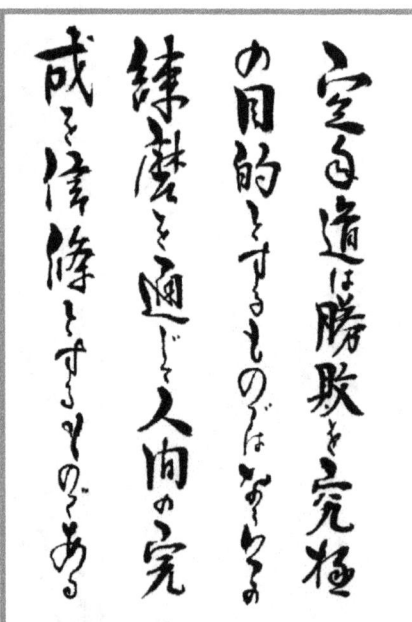

"The ultimate aim of the art of karate lies not in victory or defeat, but in the perfection of the character of its participants."
Calligraphy by Gichin Funakoshi

Perhaps the most famous book about the samurai warriors is the *Hagakure,* which means "hidden beneath the leaves."

The *Hagakure* is not written in a straightforward manner. Rather, it is written in parables and in stories and statements that, taken at face value, do not at first seem clear. The idea is that truth, itself, is not a fixed, easily discernible reality. Indeed, it is often obscured by our thoughts, emotions, educations, prejudices, and personal feelings. It usually is "hidden beneath the leaves" we see covering it, and we have to work to clear away the illusions to get down to the heart of the matter.

In one sense, this entire book is a pile of leaves.

It is easy to look at all the documents and supporting evidence, and to make judgments about who is good and who is bad, who is right and who is wrong, who is moral and who is not.

But the history and evolution of Shotokan karate-do is not that simple. There are too many people involved to simply decide that right is right and wrong is wrong. There are too many questions to be asked.

Can it be said with certainty, for example, that Hidetaka Nishiyama was acting in an irrational, autocratic way when he rejected the demands of the JKA instructors in 1978? Would it not be equally reasonable to deduce that he was, in fact, acting upon his deepest sense of moral commitment to preserve and protect the nature of karate-do as he perceived it, and was willing to suffer the repercussions, no matter how severe they might be?

Should the JKA Japanese instructors who resigned from AAKF be seen as heroes of the average student in light of their rejection of the students who later formed the AJKA? Or should they be seen as self-serving villains?

And should the Americans who formed the AJKA be seen as American citizens simply exercising their constitutional right to be free from dictatorial domination, or were they perhaps stroking their own, overblown egos, desiring to be the boss at any cost?

And what of the revered old masters mentioned throughout this book? Are we to assume that they were all of the highest moral and ethical caliber and that they would never approve of, much less engage in, the kind of political intrigues plaguing modern karate organizations?

And, finally, why would the author of this book, a person who loves and wants to promote Shotokan karate-do, expose in such detail the apparently seamy and distasteful political maneuverings of the masters he should be lauding and holding up as examples for future generations?

Ideal and Reality

The answers to all these questions—and others—lie in understanding the difference between the ideal of karate-do and the reality of karate-do.

The ideal of karate-do is that, "The ultimate aim of the art of karate lies not in victory or defeat, but in the perfection of the character of its participants." The reality of karate-do is that the participants are all human beings and that perfection of character is a continuous, lifelong process—not an end in itself.

The ideal of karate-do is to maintain a clear, everyday mind at all times and respond to everything spontaneously from the wellspring of decency and goodness within us. The reality of karate-do is that we are individual human beings, each with unique beliefs, ideas, backgrounds, and perceptions.

The ideal of karate-do is that we revere our masters and look to them for an unerring example to follow. The reality of karate-do is that both we and our masters are subject to human foibles.

In all cases, it is crucial to perceive the difference between the ideal and the reality, and not to base our judgments solely on one or the other.

This book has taken a broad, sweeping view of the history of Shotokan karate and has found some blemishes in the icon. But while it was being written, many other, significant things were happening—things that will affect the evolution of the art for generations to come.

In 1990, for example, the JKA in Japan bitterly split into two, distinct factions. One faction consisted primarily of older instructors led administratively by Nobuyuki Nakahara and technically by Motokuni Sugiura. The other faction consisted primarily of younger instructors and was led by Tetsuhiko Asai. After years of bitter fighting in the Japanese courts, the faction lead by Sugiura and Nakahara officially retained the name, Japan Karate Association, while Asai founded two organizations—the Japan Karate Shotorenmei (JKS) and the International Japan Karate Asai-ryu (IJKA).

Before the dust even settled on the Japanese court decision, more organizational splits occurred all over the world. By 2005, there were more than 20 international JKA-style technical karate organizations around the world, and numerous Shotokan-based competition organizations. Among the largest competition organizations were Hidetaka Nishiyama's ITKF (International Traditional Karate Federation) and WSKA (World Shotokan Karate Association). Some of the more successful international JKA-style technical organizations and their leaders include:

SKIF (Shotokan Karate International Federation)
Hirokazu Kanazawa
ISKF (International Shotokan Karate Federation)
Teruyuki Okazaki
WSKF (World Shotokan Karate Federation)
Hitoshi Kasuya
AJKA-I (American JKA Karate Association International)
Edmond Otis
JSKA (Japan Shotokan Karate Association)
Keigo Abe
KWF (Karatenomichi World Federation)
Mikio Yahara
FSKA (Funakoshi Shotokan Karate Association)
Kenneth Funakoshi
ISKDA (International Society of Karate-do Alliance)
Yoshikazu Sumi
WTKO (World Traditional Karate Organization)
John Mullin/Richard Amos
FBSKUI (Federation British Shotokan Karate Union International) Gerry Breeze
SSKI (Seishinkai Shotokan Karate International)
Malcolm Phipps

At this writing, all of these organizations and others appear to be healthy and growing.

On another side of the many evolutionary facets of the art in

Ideal and Reality

the U.S. stood Osamu Ozawa, for example. Ozawa was a direct pupil of Funakoshi and the original head of the Kansai branch of the JKA in Japan. When he came to the United States in 1964, he rather quickly decided that, even though he was senior to all the Japanese instructors in the U.S., he did not desire to become entangled in the politics of American karate.

For many years, Ozawa stayed out of the mainstream of JKA karate in America and quietly taught his own students. For many years he presented his Traditional Karate Tournament International in Las Vegas, Nevada, and it grew into one of the most prestigious traditional karate tournaments in the world.

Ozawa's tournament regularly attracted upwards of 2,000 contestants from all styles and from many countries. By simply pursuing his ideal independently and sincerely, he eclipsed the tournament accomplishments of the AAKF, ISKF, and AJKA combined. Following his death in 1998, the tournament was taken over by his students and is presented annually, albeit on a smaller scale than when Ozawa was alive.

The AJKA, also, underwent its own internal strife, resulting in the formation of yet another technical organization headed by Ray Dalke and Leslie Safar.

In 1994, A. R. Allen's original AJKA took a different direction entirely by changing its name to American Shotokan Karate Alliance (ASKA) and actively seeking nonrestrictive alliances with other legitimate Shotokan groups, regardless of their JKA or non-JKA lineage. The ASKA's cornerstones are "mutual respect and recognition," and the organization very quickly expanded into international alliances with many different Shotokan organizations. In fact, in 2000, the ASKA and AJKA reunited in an alliance that, while keeping the administration of the organizations independent of each other, has resulted in a mutual recognition and support of each other. Edmond Otis, Chairman of the AJKA, serves as Chairman of the ASKA Shihankai, while Randall Hassell, Chief Instructor of the ASKA, serves as President of the AJKA.

Perhaps the best lesson to be learned from the political history

Shotokan Karate: Its History and Evolution

Camp Shotokan 2000, the first combined summer camp with the American JKA Karate Association and the American Shotokan Karate Alliance. Center, behind child, is Ray Dalke. To his left is Leslie Safar, and to his right are Edmond Otis and Randall Hassell.

of JKA-style karate in the U.S. is that the art of karate-do does not lend itself readily to the constraints of strict organizational structure. Indeed, a good argument can be made for the concept that the art and the business of karate organizations should be separate.

In every case of organizational splits within the JKA structure, the problems have not arisen as a grassroots movement from among the average students. In each and every case, the problems and splits have occurred at the higher administrative levels, sometimes as a matter of principle, and sometimes as a matter of individual egos.

Following the death of Keinosuke Enoeda, Chief Instructor of the Karate Union of Great Britain (KUGB) in 2003, the JKA administration in Japan could not come to terms with the British leadership of the KUGB, and so formed yet another organization, JKA of England (JKAE). In a scenario reminiscent of the birth of the American JKA, the KUGB was forced to move forward on its own, without the support of Japan.

In a stunning replay of the actions the American JKA founders had taken against him 20 years earlier, Teruyuki Okazaki announced in April 2007 that he was leaving the JKA and that his

Ideal and Reality

ISKF would proceed on an independent course. Many of his reasons for splitting from the JKA were remarkably similar to the reasons expressed by the AJKA founders.

In a letter similar to the one he sent to the black belt students of the AJKA founders, he set a deadline, demanding that all ISKF member clubs must make an irrevocable choice between JKA membership and ISKF membership.

APRIL 2, 2007

A JOINT DECLARATION TO THE INSTRUCTORS AND MEMBERS OF THE SOUTH ATLANTIC KARATE ASSOCIATION, THE ALL-SOUTH KARATE FEDERATION, AND THE WESTERN STATES KARATE ASSOCIATION

During the second week of March, we were informed by the ISKF headquarters in Philadelphia that the ISKF had decided to pursue an independent path from JKA as of June of 2007. We, the undersigned, who comprise three of the five founding members of the ISKF, believe that our greatest strength has come from our close association with each other and our affiliations with and through the JKA.

Accordingly, we believe continued membership in the JKA is in the best interest of our clubs, our students, and our regions. Therefore, we the undersigned, after consultation with our respective regional clubs, have decided to remain members of the JKA and JKA/WF.

RESPECTFULLY,

[signature]
Mr. Takayuki Mikami, JKA

[signature and seal]
Mr. Shojiro Koyama, JKA

[signature and seal]
Mr. Shigeru Takashina, JKA

Within two weeks of his letter, three of the four senior Japanese ISKF instructors—Takayuki Mikami of Louisiana, Shojiro Koyama of Arizona, and Shigeru Takashina of Florida—announced that they were going to leave ISKF in favor of staying with the JKA. They issued a proclamation and made it publicly available for download in pdf form on the internet. Of the four senior Japanese ISKF instructors, only Yutaka Yaguchi of Colorado seemed to tilt in favor of ISKF.

What is noteworthy about all of the splits in the JKA is that in almost every single circumstance, the offshoot organizations have not only survived, but have thrived. The karate has not changed, and the leaders have not faded away from lack of attention from Japan.

Following the death of Masatoshi Nakayama in April 1987, the JKA in Japan found itself unable to immediately decide upon a new leader, and resolved instead to have the organization governed, for the time being, by committee. As one Japanese instructor put it, "If it were just a matter of picking a tough karate guy to be Chief Instructor, there wouldn't be much of a problem. But the Chief Instructor represents our art to the whole world, and he must also be able to hold a baby in his arms for a picture, and be politically sensitive. I don't think there's anybody around like that right now, so I guess we'll just concentrate on teaching in our dojo and trying to produce good students."

That is exactly what the majority of JKA-style instructors have been doing all along, and that is why the future of Shotokan karate-do is bright, and regardless of any problems along the way, the art will continue to flourish.

The ideal is a unified structure with a strong leader. The reality is the individual instructors and students, doing their best, striving toward perfection.

At the age of 70, Osamu Ozawa, a direct student of Gichin Funakoshi, was asked to reflect upon the past, present, and future of traditional karate and to explain, as he perceived it, what role karate should play in society. As a history lesson and as a vision,

Ideal and Reality

Osamu Ozawa

his profound and eloquent reply stands as an icon in understanding the history and evolution of Shotokan karate-do. Here, in his own words, is what he said:

> "Many, many books have been written about the history of karate and how it started. Some say it actually started in Greece; some say it started with a Chinese monk; and on and on. There are as many theories about the origins of karate as there are authors to write them.

"In my opinion, it doesn't matter where it started, and nobody alive today can be absolutely certain of what happened a thousand years ago. What I am certain of is that no matter where it started—Japan, China, Okinawa, Europe, or anywhere else—the matter of human survival has always hinged on the stronger and richer oppressing the weaker and poorer as a matter of survival. The weak and poor have always been victims, but they also have always had the same survival instinct as the strong and rich. Therefore, it is completely natural that oppressed people would develop some method of protecting themselves, their families, and their people.

"Wherever any martial art originated, it grew directly out of the survival instinct. Whenever and wherever life and death struggles were faced regularly, martial arts were created.

"The difference between that time and today is the difference between black and white. Survival is a much more serious matter than winning a tournament.

"The development of self-defense techniques occurred all over the world, but it seems that the particular techniques created in China became the foundation of the karate we practice today.

"In the Western world, wrestling, boxing, and fencing all grew into sports after being created to satisfy the survival instinct.

"In China, almost 400 different styles of martial arts were created over the years, and no matter what name they are called by, and no matter what their techniques look like, they all grew out of the human instinct to survive.

"Today, we look at the martial arts of China,

Ideal and Reality

Okinawa, and Japan, and we see morals and ethics. I was taught from birth about the proud morals and ethics of my samurai heritage. But the truth is that, in the beginning, there were no morals or ethics or formality. There was only survival. Even the Japanese warriors, whose descendants would become samurai, killed simply for survival.

"As generations go by, though, the world changes, and the public use for martial arts changes accordingly.

"Okinawa, such a small island in the Pacific, had very few resources, but a very advantageous location for trade between Japan, Korea, and China. Therefore, they took every opportunity to capitalize on their strategic position by trading with those countries. Since they were so small, though, they really could not mount an effective defense against outside forces, so they were always under pressure—especially from the mainland Japanese. So they had to create a way to defend themselves individually. There is no doubt that they imported some Chinese techniques and combined them with their own techniques to create the foundation of what we know as Japanese karate today.

"When Gichin Funakoshi introduced karate to Japan in 1922, Japan was already well-civilized and had many of its own martial arts, and middle class Japanese people had already studied Japan's martial arts in an educational setting that combined morals and ethics with the techniques of self-defense and survival. Martial arts were part of the Japanese educational system. Many Japanese high schools and colleges had martial art programs in place for physical education. So it was very difficult for Funakoshi Sensei to get any attention for his Okinawan art.

"However, because of his unflagging efforts, in only 75 years karate is now being taught in every corner of the world, not only for physical fitness, but as a method of character development by teaching young people the value of discipline in their mental development and the value of the technique as physical conditioning.

"After World War II and the occupation, I believe that karate became the largest single force for introducing Japanese culture to the Western world. No other part of Japanese culture—not *ikebana* (flower arranging), or *origami* (paper folding), or *cha no yu* (tea ceremony), or anything else—even comes close to comparing with karate in its influence on the West. One reason for this is that karate requires almost nothing for training—no big space or special equipment. The only thing needed is a person's own body. That's why anybody, whether young or old, man or woman, can train in karate.

"Another reason for karate's popularity in the West is that in the beginning, Westerners felt that there was some special, Oriental mystery existing in karate, and it intrigued them.

"Of course, there is no mystery at all to karate. Physically, it is like any other physical activity.

"The purpose of karate is physical conditioning, self-defense, the building of character through daily discipline, and mutual respect.

"More simply, I say to anyone who is training in karate or considering training, 'Let's use this training to make a happier life tomorrow.' Because of the way karate has developed in modern times, however, it is very difficult to attain that goal.

"In the relatively short time since the war, the popularity of karate has exploded all over the world, and the art has grown too big, too fast. Some Japanese instructors and some Westerners with experience in the art started exploiting karate's popularity for money and/or political power by controlling the millions of people wishing to train. Those instructors started organizing on a local, national, and international basis, and because of karate's popularity, their organizations grew too large, too fast. This made it impossible for the leaders to give enough benefits to the members of their organizations. At the very beginning, everybody was excited to join these organizations because the leaders had big names and great ideas, but because the foundation of these organizations was weak, the people soon started finding that there was no value in their membership. This happened both in the West and in Japan.

"I believe that staying together in one small dojo, sweating together, exchanging techniques and ideas together, is more valuable than being a member of a large organization that offers nothing in return except the honor of being associated with the leader.

"When organizations grow large, the leaders always start opposing each other. This is human nature, but it is against the nature of martial art. The leaders have made the mistake of turning their attention away from the value of karate as physical and moral education and toward karate as a vehicle for attaining money and power. This has been going on for so long that it has become a flowing stream, impossible to stop.

"When the group of young men of the Japan Karate Association organized the first sport karate tournament in 1957, they launched karate's popularity all over the world. But the old masters in Japan insisted that martial art cannot be a perfect game, and I believe that. Since the origin of martial art hinged on the life and death struggle, the rules of sport for martial arts are necessarily unclear. In judo, for example, the object is to throw the opponent to the ground, and even an untrained person can see when a good, strong throw is executed. There is no doubt that the opponent was felled and eliminated. In a life and death struggle, the outcome would be clear. But what about the contestant who struggles with his opponent and manages to get him down, but doesn't do it cleanly? In a life and death struggle, the fight would continue. But in sport, some accommodation for the contestant's effort must be provided for in the rules. Therefore, the sport must move away from the original life and death struggle in true martial art.

"In kendo, if the contestant strikes his opponent's right hand, he gets a point, but if he strikes the left hand while it is below shoulder height, nothing happens. If he was even using a bokken (wooden sword) and struck the left hand, he would be able to stop the opponent by breaking the arm. If he had a real sword, of course, he might even kill his opponent by cutting off his left hand. So, again, sport rules have removed the contestants far away from the true life and death struggle of martial art.

"So, I believe that of necessity, the rules of martial art sports are unclear and removed from the original intention of martial art training. Judgment might be clear according to the rules of a particular tournament, but in terms of a real life and death struggle, the judgment is not at all clear. This is true in all martial art contests including karate.

"On the other hand, karate tournaments are not all bad. One very good point of karate tournaments is that they help young people build a strong competitive spirit, and that can be very beneficial.

"Another positive side to tournaments is that they can lead to deep and abiding friendships. My annual tournament in Las Vegas is strongly supported by many American instructors and contestants, and this has led to some deep friendships between these people and people all over the world.

"Also, a tournament is an opportunity to educate the public on the subject of karate and to bring students and instructors of varied backgrounds together. Each year, my tournament in Las Vegas is spread over three days and includes Master Clinics conducted by some of the highest-ranking, most highly qualified karate instructors in the world. Beginning with the 1988 tournament at the Riviera Hotel, I decided to spend approximately $5,000 on the opening 10 minutes of the finals. I designed this opening with sound, lighting, shadow, music, and movement. Some critics have said that it is just a show, and I confess that it is, indeed, a show. But it is a show that educates the public about the history and meaning of karate training. A good demonstration, I believe, should be a good show. If it is interesting and tasteful, the audience will be interested in it, and they will remember it. I believe that the majority of karate demonstrations also are a show, but they often are too much pre-arranged and stilted.

"My annual tournament is one of the largest traditional karate tournaments in the world, and I am happy to see the great spirit displayed by the young people who compete in it. But I have no intention of conducting any more tournaments than I do now or trying to greatly expand my efforts. There are so many tournaments around the world now, that there is no need for more. In the United States alone, there are at least 2,000 karate tournaments each year. Those tournaments produce 2,000 champions and that, I believe, is more than enough.

"Because large organizations have so strongly promoted tournaments, the stream has now become a raging river.

"For the past 20 years, the main thrust of the leaders of sport karate has been the effort to have karate accepted as an Olympic sport. The efforts of the various international leaders to get karate into the Olympics have been extraordinary. I doubt that anybody has worked harder for a cause than these men have for more than 20 years. The problem is that the leaders have been competing against each other for Olympic recognition rather than pulling together and unifying their efforts. This struggle for Olympic recognition, I believe, has been the culprit in turning karate more away from its roots as a martial art and more toward sport competition.

"I believe that roosters in a cockfight are better fighters than most of today's karate tournament fighters, and I believe it is time for everybody—leaders and instructors—to carefully re-think the whole business of karate. Rather than train students strictly for tournaments, I think we should all get back to the fundamentals. While maintaining strict control of their techniques, the students should be taught with the actual intention to hit their opponent. Each attack should be strong and consequential. This method might take longer to develop free sparring skills in the students, but the time is worth it because it truly teaches them how to defend themselves. It makes both the attacker and the defender more cautious and more serious.

"The leaders and instructors of the next generation of karate practitioners must seek ways to respect the traditional ways and still create a good sport. No matter what happens, both traditional karate training as a martial art and modern karate training as a sport will move forward, and neither one can be stopped. It would be a waste of time to try to stop them. Their best hope-and challenge-is to find a way to create a good combination of the two for the benefit of the millions of people training in karate.

"Many people today say that karate techniques and karate training methods have changed. Yes, they have, but I don't think anyone can say with certainty that these changes have been bad or good. Changes from generation to generation are natural and unstoppable in all areas of life—not just in karate. Things change because the world changes and people change. Whether we like it or not, we must face the reality of change. Still, the one thing we must not forget is the true purpose of karate training.

"Because modern karate originated in Japan, Japanese karate leaders believe that Japanese karate is superior to all others. I personally believe that in the 50 years the West has had to learn karate, they have become equal with the Japanese in knowledge, technique, and teaching ability. A young Western instructor is completely equal in ability to a young Japanese instructor. The only thing lacking in the Western instructor is the fact that he is not Japanese. The Japanese believe that because they are Japanese, they have some kind of special understanding of karate that Westerners don't have. I question that kind of thinking, and I challenge the idea that it is even important. At this moment in history, the world looks to the Japanese as superior karate people because the art has been transmitted to the world by the Japanese. But everybody, especially the Japanese, seems to have forgotten that the techniques of this art were transmitted to Japan from Okinawa and China. Who, I would like to ask, is looking to the Okinawans and Chinese as superior, simply because they transmitted an art to Japan? Certainly not the Japanese! Karate people in Japan do not look at the Okinawans and Chinese as the rest of the karate world looks today at Japan.

"As the Okinawans taught karate to the mainland Japanese, and the Japanese took that teaching and transformed it into their own karate, so will the rest of the world. I believe that in about two more generations, each country will take what they have learned from the Japanese and make their own karate, exactly like the Japanese did. I believe this is natural, unstoppable, and necessary. My one hope is that the traditional principles of karate will be preserved.

Ideal and Reality

"I believe that the next generation will combine tradition and sport. The leaders must seek what is most beneficial for the people. And who will these leaders be? They will be the leaders who are teaching on a daily basis in the dojo, without any political motive. Those individual instructors are the true leaders of karate. They always have been, and they always will be, regardless of what the heads of large organizations believe. Just as the origin of karate techniques lies in the life and death struggle, the origin of karate transmission lies in the *uchi-deshi* system. *Uchi-deshi* means "inside or direct student" and implies that transmission of the art is from one sensei to one student, and that the transmission is direct, personal, and private. The more we have moved toward sport, the more we have moved away from the original *uchi-deshi* method. Of course, once karate was opened to the public in Okinawa, the true uchi-deshi method was no longer possible because many people started participating in a group setting. Still, the transmission of true karate was from one instructor to his small group of students, and that is the way we must think when we teach.

"People who think the leaders of karate are the heads of large international organizations are wrong. Some people with great responsibility in those international organizations have extremely limited knowledge of karate, and some have none at all. Political leadership, after all, does not require expert knowledge of karate. The true leaders of karate, I believe, are the unknown and unsung heroes who daily dedicate themselves to teaching the true meaning of karate to their own small group of students. These instructors are the ones who will determine where karate will go in the future, because it is they who will teach the students how to act and how to train. True teachers don't have to be well known, like political leaders; they just have to be dedicated.

"My sensei, Gichin Funakoshi, said, *"Shoshin wasu re be ka ra zu,"* which means, "Do not forget the initial intention when you started." In other words, if you want to be a good karate teacher, remember how you felt on the first day you started training. I don't think he was telling us to be overly or falsely humble, but I do think he wanted us to remember our humble beginnings so that we would train harder to teach better and to at least have some compassion for our students. As soon as anyone gets to be too much of a big shot, they should think about these words from Funakoshi Sensei, and they should go back to their own dojo and their own people and rediscover their roots.

"I do not know what the true future of karate will be, because when I look back to karate in Japan before the war, I remember that it was utterly unthinkable that karate would ever be a huge, popular, worldwide art with millions of practitioners. But look at what happened.

"I can't know, so I hope. I hope that everybody will cling to their roots and go back to their own dojos and take care of their own people. I hope they will think deeply about the benefit of karate training for their own students. And I hope that all karate people will take advantage of every opportunity to gather together and exchange techniques and ideas among themselves, regardless of style or school or affiliation.

"Some national and international leaders

today seem to have the attitude that, 'Karate is mine. I own it. If you want to learn karate, come to me. I'm the true way to go.' This idea is completely wrong, and it must be eradicated. I believe it will be eradicated as more and more instructors realize how wrong it is and return to their roots for the benefit of their people."[1]

Epilogue

Finally, I leave the reader with the words of Gichin Funakoshi. These are called Shoto Niju Kun, or Shoto's 20 Precepts. My teachers told me that Master Funakoshi said much more in these 20 phrases than I will ever be able to say in a lifetime and, the more I study, the more I believe they are right.

These precepts are the subject of another (or several) volume(s). Until that time, they are offered with the cautions that 1) simple translations are utterly inadequate, and 2) the more they are studied, the more their meaning will change.

Shoto Niju Kun
(Shoto's Twenty Precepts)

1. Karate-do wa rei ni hajimari, rei ni owaru koto wo wasuruna.
(Karate-do begins with courtesy and ends with courtesy.)

2. Karate ni sente nashi.
(There is no first attack in karate.)

3. Karate wa gi no tasuke.
(Karate is a great assistance to [auxilliary of] justice.)

4. Mazu jiko wo shire, shikoshite tao wo shire.
(Know yourself first, and then others.)

5. Gijutsu yori shinjutsu.
(Spirit first; techniques second.)

6. **Kokoro wa hanatan koto wo yosu.**
   (Always be ready to release your mind.)
7. **Wazawai wa getai ni shozu.**
   (Misfortune [accidents] always comes out of idleness [negligence].)
8. **Dojo nomino karate to omou na.**
   (Do not think that karate training is only in the dojo.)
9. **Karate no shugyo wa issho de aru.**
   (It will take your entire life to learn karate; there is no limit.)
10. **Araiyuru mono wo karateka seyo, soko ni myo-mi ari.**
    (Put your everyday living into karate and you will find the ideal state of existence *[myo].*)
11. **Karate wa yu no goto shi taezu natsudo wo ataezareba moto no mizu ni kaeru.**
    (Karate is like hot water. If you do not give it heat constantly, it will again become cold water.)
12. **Katsu kangae wa motsu na makenu kangae wa hitsuyo.**
    (Do not think that you have to win. Rather, think that you do not have to lose.)
13. **Tekki ni yotte tenka seyo.**
    (Victory depends on your ability to distinguish vulnerable points from invulnerable ones.)
14. **Tattakai wa kyojutsu no soju ikan ni ari.**
    (The battle is according to how you maneuver guarded and unguarded. Move according to your opponent.)
15. **Hito no te ashi wo ken to omoe.**
    (Think of the hands and feet as swords.)
16. **Danshi mon wo izureba hyakuman no tekki ari.**
    (When you leave home, think that you have numerous opponents waiting for you. It is your behavior that invites trouble from them.)

17. Kamae wa shoshinsha ni ato wa shizentai.
(Beginners must master low stance and posture; natural body position for advanced.)

18. Kata wa tadashiku jissen wa betsu mono.
(Practicing a kata is one thing, and engaging in a real fight is another.

19. Chikara no kyojaku, karada no shinshuku, waza no kankyu wo wasaruna.
(Do not forget [1] strength and weakness of power, [2] stretching and contraction of the body, and [3] slowness and speed of techniques. Apply these correctly.)

20. Tsune ni shinen kufu seyo.
(Always think and devise ways to live the precepts every day.)

Notes

Chapter 1
[1] Quoted in Ohtomo, Shuho. "Kanshi and Shodo," *Samurai*, Summer, 1971, p. 41.

Chapter 3
[1] Funakoshi, Gichin. Quoted in translation in *Karate-Do, My Way of Life*. Tokyo: Kodansha International Ltd., 1977, pp. 77–78.
[2] Hassell, Randall G. *Conversations With the Master: Masatoshi Nakayama*. St. Louis, Focus Publications, 1983.
[3] Ibid.
[4] Ibid.

Chapter 4
[1] Hassell, Randall G. "An Interview With Hidetaka Nishiyama." *Samurai*, Autumn, 1978. pp. 12–17; 27–29.
[2] Op. cit.
[3] Ibid.
[4] Ibid.
[5] Nishiyama, Hidetaka. "The Karate Contest." *Samurai*, Vol. 1, No. 2, 1972, p. 34.

Chapter 5
1 Op. cit.
2 Ibid.
3 Rosenthal, Jim. "The Legacy of Gichin Funakoshi, An Interview with Tsutomu Ohshima." *Black Belt,* September, 1987. pp. 51–52.

Chapter 7
1 Hassell, Randall G. and Ozawa, Osamu. *Samurai Journey.* St. Louis, Focus Publications, 1997.

Appendix A

The Origins of Shotokan Karate Kata

NAME	MEANING	COMMENTS
Heian (1–5)	Peaceful	Originally named Pinan, with 1 and 2 reversed in order. Created by Y. Itosu for use in PE classes in 1905. Heian is a contraction of *Heiwa-antei* (peace and calmness).
Tekki (1)	Horse Riding	Very old Shuri-te *kata*, also called Naihanchi or Iron Horse.
Tekki (2 & 3)	Modeled after Tekki 1, and created by Y. Itosu.	
Bassai Dai	To Penetrate a Fortress	One of the oldest *kata*; also called Patsai, Patasai or Passai. Common in various forms in many styles, and can be traced back at least to Oyadomari.

Kanku Dai	Sky Viewing	Ancient Shurite *kata*, common in various forms in many styles. Originally named after Kung Siang Chun (Koshokun in Japanese), a Chinese envoy to Okinawa during the Ming dynasty. Also commonly called Kwanku, Koshokun, and Kushanku.
Jion	A Proper Name or Temple Bell	Ancient Tomari-te *kata*, possibly brought from the Jion temple in China to Tomari. Widely practiced in Shotokan and Wado-ryu.
Jutte	Ten Hands	Tomari-te *kata* which may also be performed with a staff in the hands. Today, the empty-hand version is unique to Shotokan.
Empi	Flying Swallow	Ancient *kata* originally called Wanshu, and traceable to the 18th Century. Transmitted from Sanaeda and Matsumora to Sokon Matsumura. Practiced extensively in Tomari and developed by Kiyatake, its present form comes from Y. Itosu.

Hangetsu	Crescent Moon	Naha-te *kata* originally called Seishan. The name, Hangetsu, describes the crescent-like stepping pattern exhibited in the kata.
Gankaku	Crane on a Rock	Originally called Chinto. Taught to Sokon Matsumura by Matsumora. Kyatake Chinto (which features sagi-ashi dachi, or the sole of one foot resting against the inner knee of the opposite leg) is widely practiced in many styles, while Itosu's Chinto (Gankaku), which features gankaku dachi (foot hooked behind the knee) is practiced only in Shotokan and Shito-ryu.
Bassai Sho	The Lesser Bassai	Created by Y. Itosu, using Bassai Dai as a model.
Kanku Sho	The Lesser Kanku	Created by Y. Itosu, using Kanku Dai as a model.
Gojushiho Dai	The Greater 54 Directions	Originally called Useshi, and renamed by Funakoshi as Hotaku. A Shuri-te *kata* taught by Y. Itosu and favored by Kenwa Mabuni and Kanken Toyama, it is

		today an advanced *kata* of both Shotokan and Shito-ryu.
Gojushiho Sho	The Lesser 54 Directions	A variation of Gojushiho Dai.
Chinte	Unusual (Strange) Hands	Also called Shoin, and believed to be an ancient Chinese *kata*. Practiced today in Shotokan and Shito-ryu.
Sochin	Immovable or Rooted	Probably created by Ankichi Arakaki, and originally called Hakko. Changed extensively by Yoshitaka Funakoshi, it is practiced today primarily in Shotokan and Shito-ryu.
Nijushiho	24 Directions	Originally called Niseshi, and probably created by Ankichi Arakaki. Practiced today in Shotokan, Shito-ryu, and Wado-ryu.
Unsu	Hands in the Clouds	Considered the most advanced *kata* in Shotokan, it contains elements from 15 different *kata*, and can be traced to Ankichi Arakaki.

Ji'in	Temple Grounds	A Tomari-te *kata* originally called Shokyo.
Meikyo	Polished Mirror	Originally called Rohai and divided into three separate *kata*, Meikyo may also be performed with a staff in the hands. Not taught extensively by Funakoshi, perhaps because it contains *sankaku-tobi* (triangular leap), which in old times was held to be a secret and spiritual technique.
Wankan	King's Crown	Also called Hito and Shiofu. A very old *kata* of Tomari-te, traceable as far back as Matsumora. Practiced today in Shotokan and Shito-ryu.

Appendix B

The 15 Basic Kata of Shotokan Karate and Their Technical Value

Listed below are the 15 *kata* that Gichin Funakoshi brought to Japan in 1922 as the foundation of his karate, and the main physical value of the kata.

Name	Main Points to be Learned
Heian 1	Front stance, back stance, stepping patterns, lunge punch.
Heian 2	Front kick, side kick while changing directions.
Heian 3	Body connections in forearm blocking, back-fist strike.
Heian 4	Balance; variation in techniques.
Heian 5	Balance and jumping.
Tekki 1	Straddle-leg stance, hip vibration.
Tekki 2	Grasping and hooking blocks.

Tekki 3	Continuous middle-level blocking.
Bassai Dai	Changing disadvantage into advantage by use of switching blocks and differing degrees of power.
Kanku Dai	Variation in fast and slow techniques; jumping.
Jion	Turning, shifting variations in stepping patterns.
Jutte	Powerful hip action, use of the staff.
Empi	Fast and slow movements, high and low body positions, reversal of body positions.
Hangetsu	Inside tension stance; coordination of breathing with stepping, blocking and punching; circular arm and leg movements.
Gankaku	Balancing on one leg; side kick; back-fist strike.

Gichin Funakoshi's
Three Cardinal Principles of Kata

1. Power Control
   (Chikara No Kyojaku)

2. Expansion and Contraction of Muscles
   (Karada No ShinShiku)

3. Speed and Rhythm Control
   (Waza No Kamkyu)

Appendix C

The Genealogy of Modern Karate

Shuri-te/Naha-te Family Tree

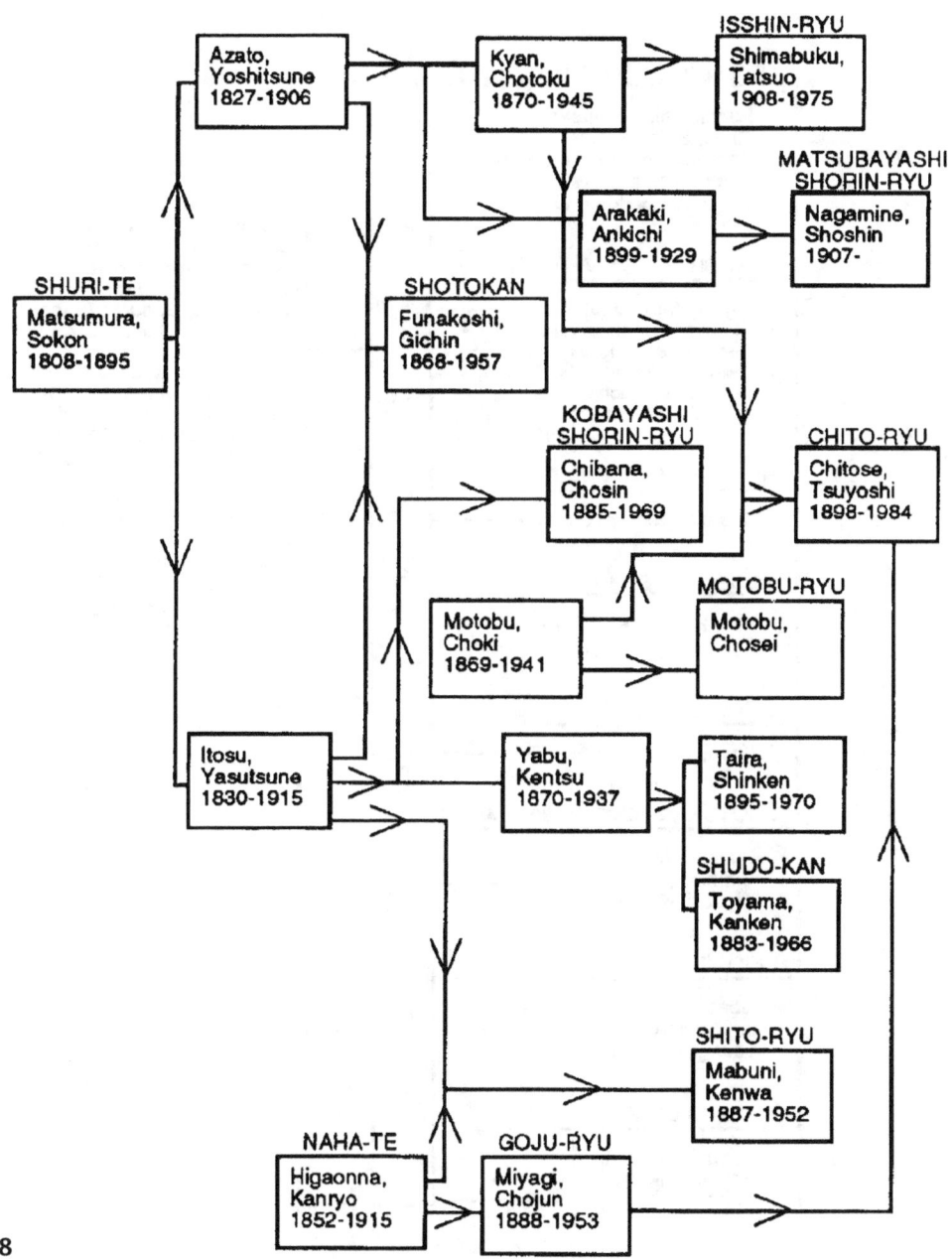

Shotokan Karate-do Family Tree

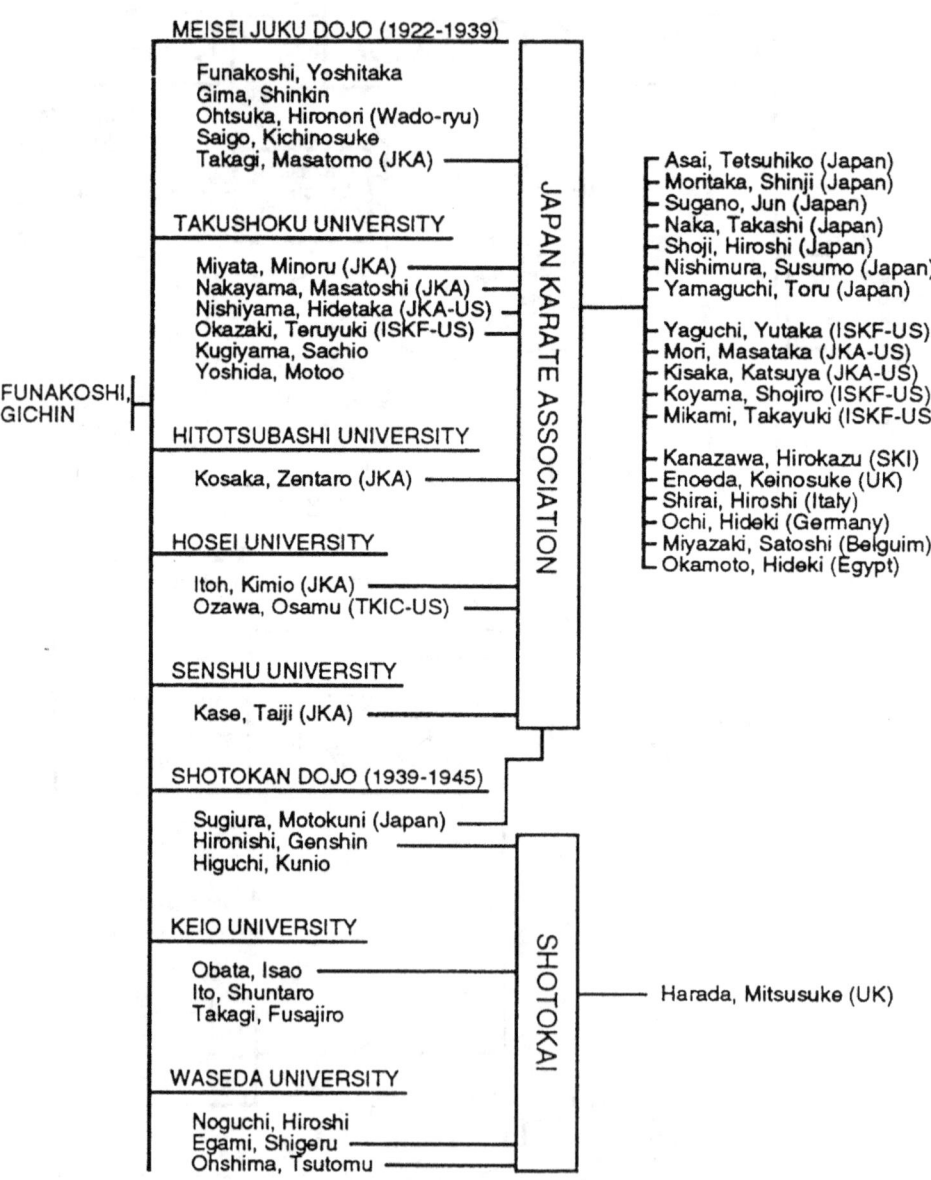

U.S. First Generation JKA Instructors
(Active in 1990)

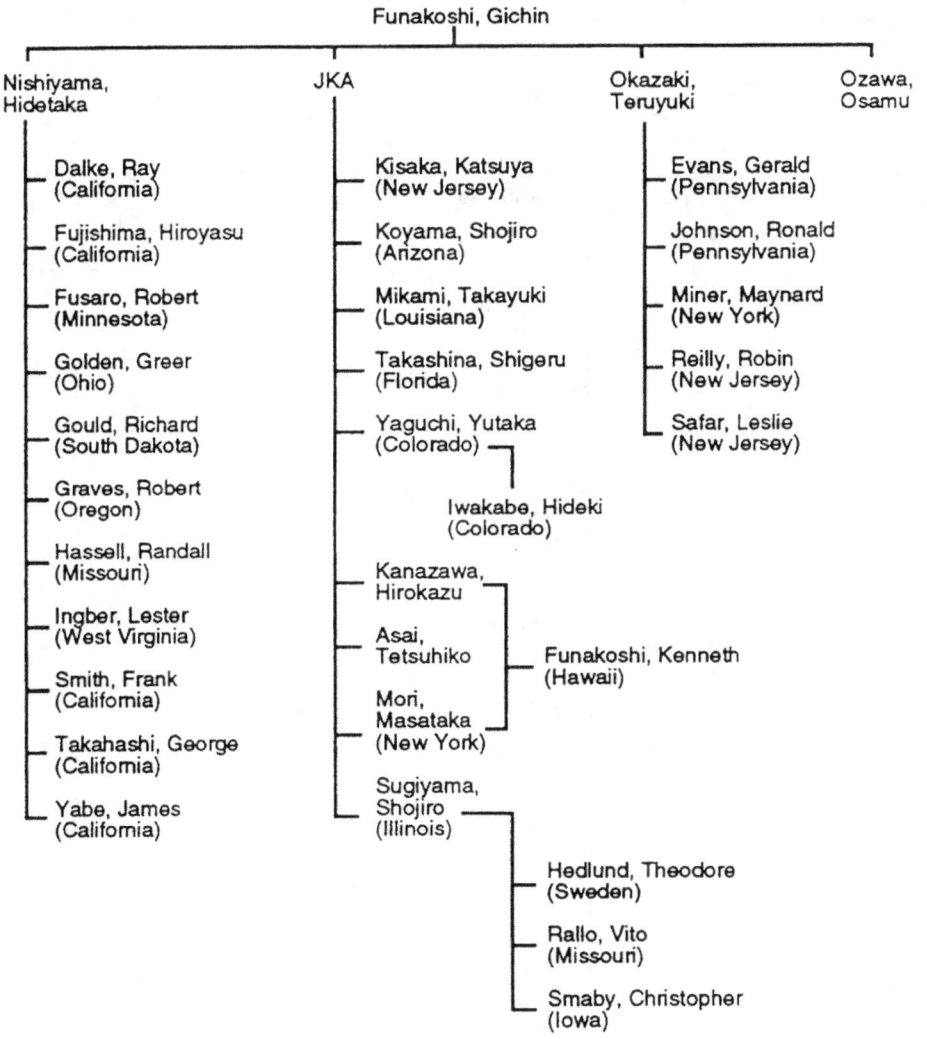

European Karate Family Tree

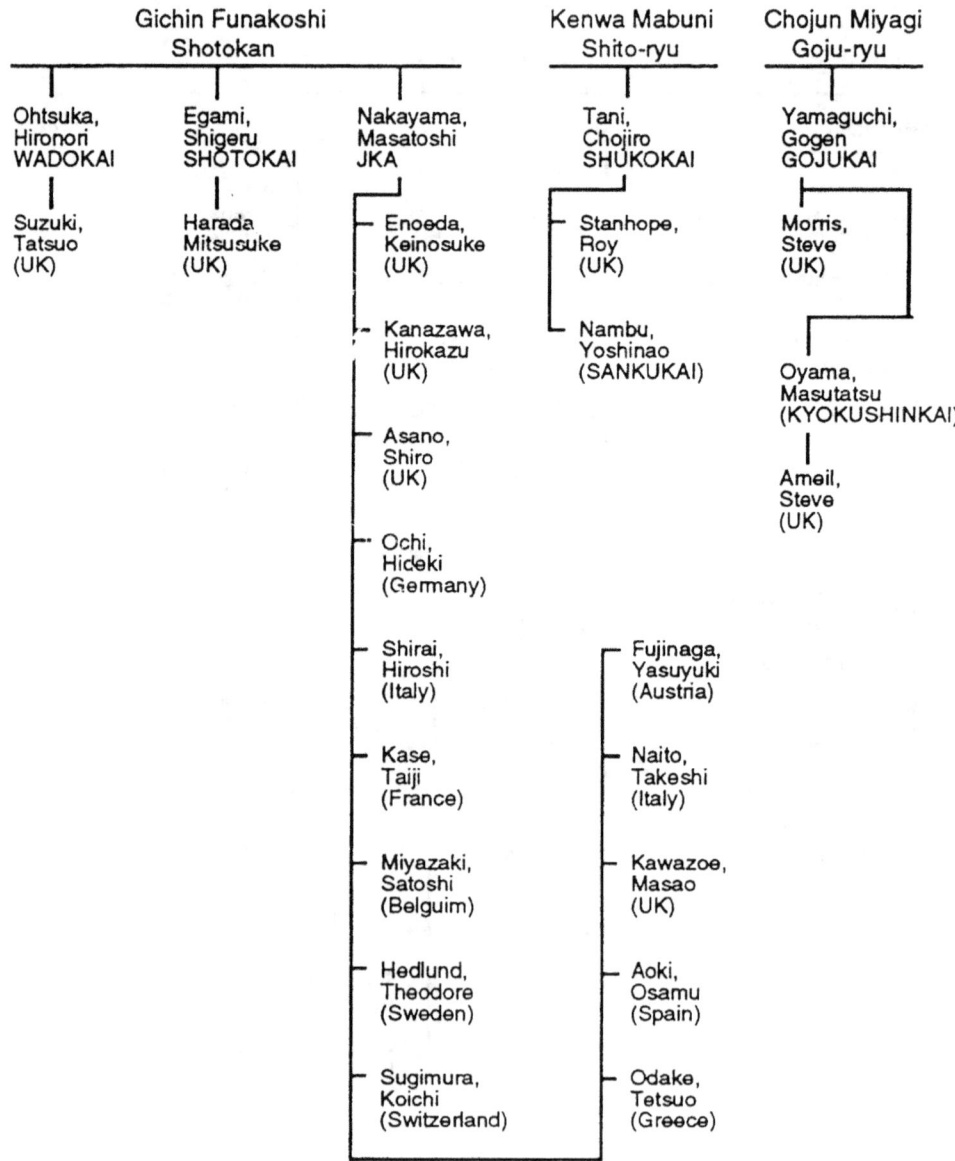

Gichin Funakoshi Shotokan			Kenwa Mabuni Shito-ryu	Chojun Miyagi Goju-ryu
Ohtsuka, Hironori WADOKAI	Egami, Shigeru SHOTOKAI	Nakayama, Masatoshi JKA	Tani, Chojiro SHUKOKAI	Yamaguchi, Gogen GOJUKAI
Suzuki, Tatsuo (UK)	Harada Mitsusuke (UK)	Enoeda, Keinosuke (UK)	Stanhope, Roy (UK)	Morris, Steve (UK)
		Kanazawa, Hirokazu (UK)	Nambu, Yoshinao (SANKUKAI)	
		Asano, Shiro (UK)		Oyama, Masutatsu (KYOKUSHINKAI)
		Ochi, Hideki (Germany)		Ameil, Steve (UK)
		Shirai, Hiroshi (Italy)	Fujinaga, Yasuyuki (Austria)	
		Kase, Taiji (France)	Naito, Takeshi (Italy)	
		Miyazaki, Satoshi (Belguim)	Kawazoe, Masao (UK)	
		Hedlund, Theodore (Sweden)	Aoki, Osamu (Spain)	
		Sugimura, Koichi (Switzerland)	Odake, Tetsuo (Greece)	

Wado-ryu Family Tree

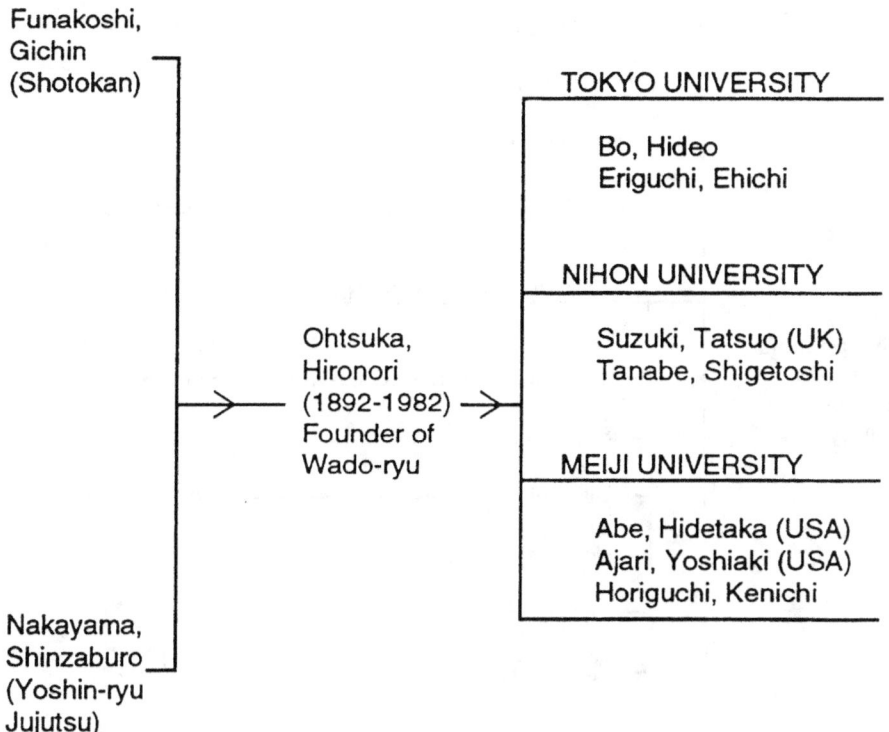

Goju-ryu Family Tree

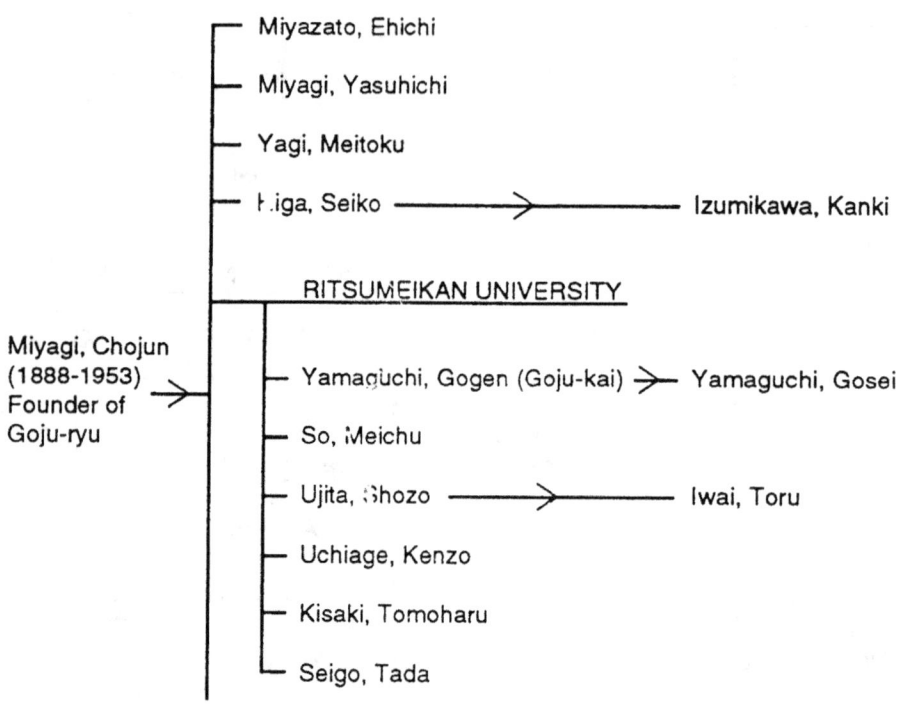

Shito-ryu Family Tree

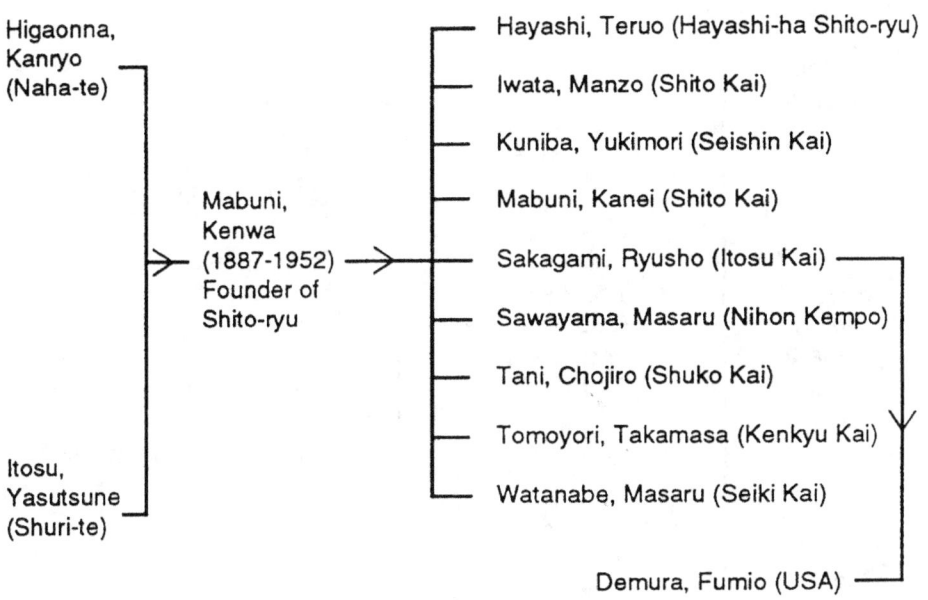

Chito-ryu Family Tree

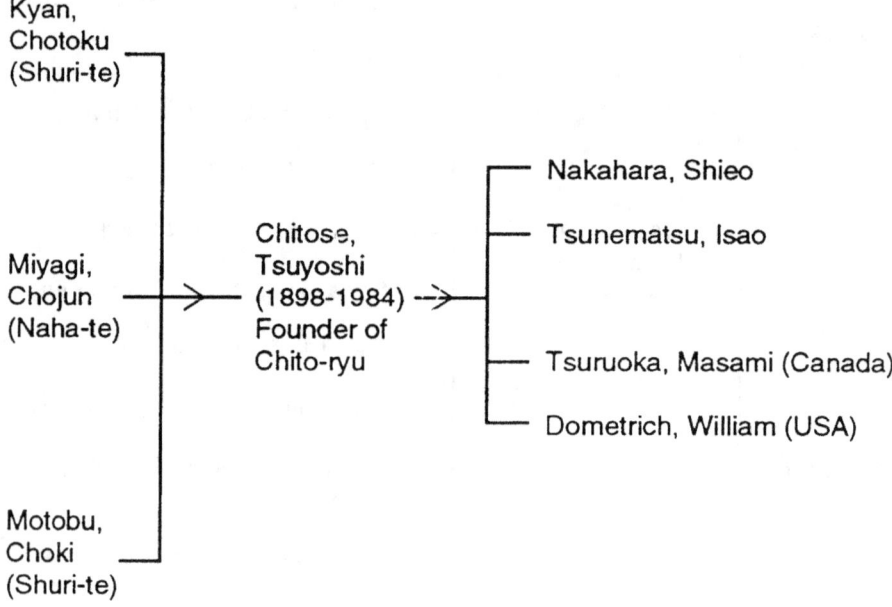

Kyokushinkai Family Tree

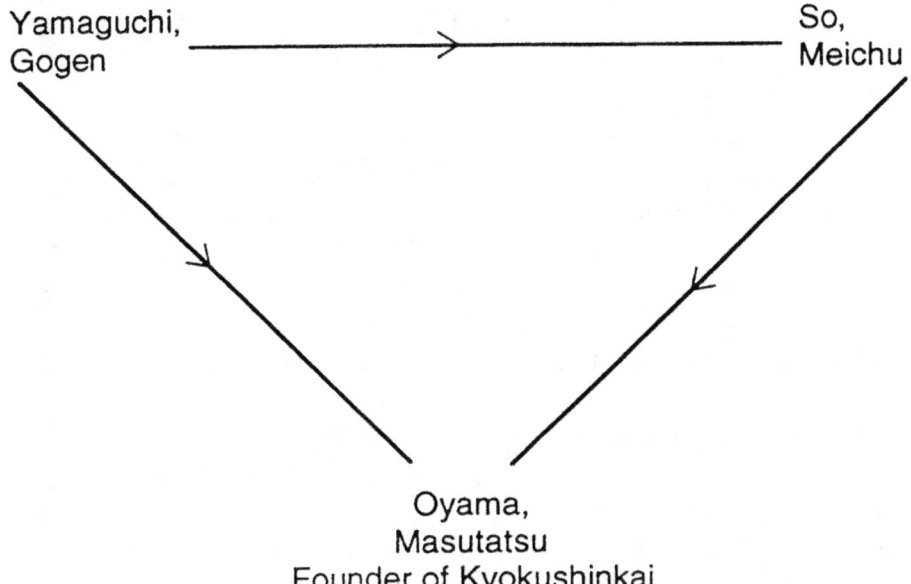

Index

A Full Determination (see *Ji Fun Shi*)
A New Method for Teaching Karate-do (see *Karate-do Shinkyotei*)
AAKF (see All America Karate Federation, American Amateur Karate Federation)
AAKF Collegiate Karate Union 97, 101
AAU (see Amateur Athletic Union)
aikido, 55, 86, 89
Ajari, Yoshiaki, 90, 91
AJKA (see American JKA Karate Associations)
All America Karate Federation (see also American Amateur Karate Federation), 95, 98, 100, 101, 107, 128
All Japan Collegiate Karate Union, 45
All Japan Karate-do Association 85-86
All Japan Karate-do Championship Tournament, 77, 82, 98
All Japan Kempo Federation, 39

Allen, A. R., v, 102, 103, 109, 110, 112, 133, 136-139, 147
Amateur Athletic Union of the United States, 97-100, 102-104, 107-110, 114, 126, 137
American Amateur Karate Federation (see also All America Karate Federation), 93, 96-97, 102-109, 113-114, 126, 129, 130, 132-134, 137, 144, 147
American JKA Karate Associations, vi, 97, 134-138, 140-141, 144, 146-149
American Shotokan Karate Alliance, vi, 147
Aoki, Osamu, 115
Arabia, 3
Arakaki, Ankichi, 174
Armed Forces Karate Association, 97, 101
Armstrong, Steve, 90
arrow (see *ya*)
arts of weaponry (see *kobudo*)
Asai, Tetsuhiko, 93, 94, 145
ASKA (see American Shotokan Karate Alliance)

Auerbach, Phillip, 100
ax (see masakari)
Azato, Yasutsune, 6, 23-26

B-47 aircraft, 86
Bangkok, Thailand, 81
basic sparring (see kihon kumite)
Bassai Dai, vi, 37, 58, 60, 169, 171, 175
Bassai Sho, 37, 60, 171
Black Belt magazine, 120, 141, 168
bo, 7, 8, 9
bo-jutsu, 9
bolo (see suruchin)
bow (see yumi)
Brooks, John, 106
Bruno, Emilio, 55, 56, 86, 87
Buddhists (see Zen Buddhists)
budo, 33, 68
Butokuden, 28, 33
Byrd, George, 111

Cardinal Principles of Kata, 176
chikaraishi, 17
China, 2-3, 6, 15, 50, 63-66, 120, 152, 153, 160, 170
Chinese boxing, 5, 15, 64-65, 67
Chinte, 37, 172
Chinto (see Gankaku)
Chito-ryu, 91
Cho, S. Henry, 90

Chuo University, 39, 117
Chuzan kingdom, 2-3
Confucianism, 24
court nobles (see kuge)
Crown Prince (see Hirohito, Emperor)
Cwiklowski, Ed, 90

Dai Nippon Butokukai, 33, 41
Dai Nippon Butokukai Bujustu Semmon Gakko, 33
Dai Nippon Kempo Karate-do, 50
Daiichi Sogo Bank, 37
Daimyo, 23
Dalke, Ray, 71, 95, 97, 100, 133-136, 138-139, 141, 147-148
Demura, Fumio, 91
Draeger, Donn, 91

East Coast Karate Association, 93
Ebata, Hidetoshi, 115
Ebisu, 68
Education, Department of (Okinawa), 25
Education, Ministry of (Japan) 26-29, 33, 67, 68, 78
Egami, Shigeru, 117-119
eku, 8
Empi, 58, 161, 170, 175
empty-handed, 3, 6
Enoeda, Keinosuke, 95, 115, 116, 148

Equinoa, Constantine, 100
Eriguchi, Ehichi, 99, 110
Evans, Gerald, 95
FAJKO (see Federation of All Japan Karate-do Organizations)
Far East University, 83
Federation of All Japan Karate-do Organizations, 80
Field, James, 95
five-step sparring (see gohon kumite)
Foochow, China, 1
free sparring (see jiyu kumite)
Fujikawa, Rei, 100
Funakoshi, Yoshitaka (Giko), 46, 54, 60-61, 119, 120, 172
Fusaro, Robert, 94, 96, 124

Gakashuin University, 72
Gankaku, 58, 61, 171, 175
Gehlsen, John, 111
General Headquarters of Allied Powers, 66-67
gentry class (see shizoku class)
geta (see tetsugeta)
gifuku, 25
Gima, Shinkin, 34, 87
gohon kumite, 43, 45
Goju-ryu, 15, 40, 42, 61, 62, 86, 90, 183
Gojushiho, 37, 58, 61, 171, 172
Golden, Greer, 95

Goto, Prince Shimpei, 36
Gould, Richard, 134
Graves, Robert, 95, 96, 102
Great Kanto Earthquake, 37
Greater Khingan Mountains, 64

Habu, Yoshiaki, 115
Hagakure, 143
Hakko (see Sochin)
halberd (see naginata)
Half-heart (see Hanko)
Hall of Shoto (see Shotokan, the)
hand (see te)
hand implements (see te gua)
hand-held weights (see sashi)
handle (see tonfa)
Hangetsu, 58, 61, 171, 175
Hanko (see also Shito-ryu), 52
Hassell, Randall G. vi, 124, 126, 133, 138, 139, 147, 148
Hayashi, Teruo, 41, 42
Heian kata, vi, 37, 58, 169, 174
Heian Shrine, 33
Heiwa-ante (see Heian kata)
hera, 13
Hien Karate-uchi, 80
Higaonna, Kanryo, 15, 39-40
Higashino, Tetsuma, 115
Hirohito, Emperor, 28
Hironishi, Genshin, 117-119
Hiroshima, 61

Hisamasa, Prince, 36
Hito (see Wankan)
Hitotsubashi University
 (see Shodai University)
hitotsuki, hitogeri, 26
Hokkaido Region (see JKA,
 Hokkaido Region)
Hokuzan kingdom, 2
Hosei University, 39, 68,
 72, 73

iaido, 38
IAKF (see International
 Amateur Karate
 Federation)
igen, 24
ikken hisatsu, 22, 45
Imperial Household Agency, 38
Inouye, Mitsuo, 115
Instructor Training Program
 (JKA), 78, 83, 123
International Amateur Karate
 Federation, 109-111,
 113-114, 128-129
International Shotokan Karate
 Federation, 93, 115,
 132-137, 140, 146-147,
 149-150
International Traditional Karate
 Federation, 146
iron clogs (see *tetsugeta*)
ISKF (see International
 Shotokan Karate
 Federation)
Isshin-ryu, 90

ITKF (see International
 Traditional Karate
 Federation
Itoh, Kimio, 71, 99, 129,
 139, 140
Itosu, Yasutsune, 6, 24, 26-28,
 39, 40, 58, 169, 170, 171
Iwata, Manzo, 99

Java, 3
Ji Fun Shi, 31
Ji'in, 37, 175
Jichi Hall, 38
Jion, 37, 58, 172
Johnson, Ronald, 95
judo, 14, 33-35, 43, 49, 55,
 66-67, 74, 85-89, 156
jujutsu, 41
Jumu, 37
jutsu, 14
Jutte, 37, 58, 172, 178
jyu kumite (free sparring),
 44-45, 74-75, 94, 159
jyu-ippon kumite, 44

Kagoshima Prefecture, 26
kakete-biki, 18
Kaloudis, Edward, 90
kama, 9,10,12
Kamata, Toshiro, 55, 56, 87
kame, 17
Kanazawa, Hirokazu, 72, 82,
 83, 93, 117, 125, 132, 146
kanda, 12
Kanku, 5

Kanku Dai, 27, 34, 37, 59, 170, 171, 175
Kanku Sho, 37, 60, 173
Kanna, Norikazu, 36
Kano, Jigoro, 34, 35, 51
kanshu, 18-19
kara, 14, 50
Karate ni sente nashi, 36, 164
Karate-Do (film), 81
Karate-do Goju-Kai, 86
Karate-do Kyohan, 44, 46, 49, 119, 120
karate-jutsu, 15, 19, 42
Kase, Taiji, 115, 116
Kasuya, Shinyo, 39
katana, 2
Kataoka Movie Center, 72
Kawazoe, Masao, 115
Keio University, 39, 55, 67, 68, 72, 73, 90, 92, 117, 120
Keio University Research Group 50
Kelly, John B., 98
kendo, 14, 33, 38, 43, 49, 74, 75, 85, 156
Kenshin-ryu, 42
kihon kumite (basic sparring), 44
kihon-ippon kumite, 44
Kim, Richard, 103, 111
King, Everett L., 136
Kisaka, Katsuya, 94, 115
Kisarazu AFB, 85
Kiyatake, 172
Kiyuna, 24

kizoku, 23
Kobayashi Shorin-ryu, 15
kobudo, 6
Kodokan, 34, 35, 55, 86, 87, 88
Koei-Kan, 86, 90
Koishikawa, 54
Kokan, 37
kokangeiko, 74
Kokuba, Kosei, 42
Kondo, Minako, 115
Konishi, Yasuhiro, 41, 116
Korea, 2, 3, 153
Kosaka, Zentaro, 129, 132
Koshokun (see Kun, Siang Chun)
Koshokun kata (see Kanku Dai/Kanku Sho)
Kosugi, Hoan, 35, 37, 51
Kotani, Sumiyaki, 55, 87
Koyama, Shojiro, 94, 95, 115, 127, 150
kuge, 23
kumade, 13
Kumemura settlement, 4-5
Kung, Siang Chun, 4
kung-fu, 90
Kuniba, Kosei (see Kokuba, Kosei)
Kuntoku Daiku Goten shrine, 25
kusarigama, 10
Kushanku (see Kanku Dai/Kanku Sho)
Kwanku (see Kanku Dai/Kanku Sho)

191

Kyan, Chotoku, 27
Kyoto, 28, 33, 61, 69
Kyushu, 1, 3, 54

lever bar (see kakete-biki)
Liu Liu Ko, 26
long oar (see eku)
long staff (see bo)

Mabuni, Kenwa, 27, 39, 40, 61, 62, 78
Machida, Yoshizo, 115
Mademoiselle magazine, 80
makiage-gu, 17, 18
makiwara, 16, 18, 19, 43, 119
Malacca, 3
Manchuria, 64
Martial Virtues Hall (see Butokuden)
masakari, 13
Matsubayashi Shorin-ryu, 86
Matsumora, 170, 171, 173
Matsumura, Sokon ("Bushi"), 6, 24, 28, 60, 170, 171
Matsuzakaya Department Stores, 38
Mattson, George, 90
Meiji Restoration, 14, 23
Meiji University, 39
Meikyo, 58, 175
Meisei Juku, 36, 37
Men's Normal School, 26
Mikami, Takayuki, 82, 83, 93, 115, 124, 126, 127, 150
Minamoto clan, 2

Miner, Maynard, 95
Ming Dynasty, 4, 5, 173
Mirakian, Anthony, 90
Miyagi, Chojun, 15, 40
Miyata, Minoru, 69, 119, 120
Miyazaki, Satoshi, 115
Mori, Masataka, 93, 115
Motobu, Choki, 27, 41

Nagamine, Shoshin, 86
naginata, 2, 10
Nagle, Don, 90
Naha, 4, 15
Naha City School of Commerce, 40
Naha-te, 39, 173
Naihanchi (see Tekki kata)
Naito, Takeshi, 115
Nakahara, Nobuyuki, 145
Nakayama, Hakudo, 38
Nakayama, Masatoshi, v., 42, 45, 48, 53, 55, 56, 58, 63, 67, 71-75, 78, 80-81, 83, 85, 87-88, 99, 115, 119-120, 129, 134, 150
Nanzan kingdom, 2
National Athletic Exhibition, 29, 33, 35
National Collegiate Athletic Association (NCAA), 109
National Railroad Company, 67
nichigama, 10
Nihon University, 39
Niigaki, 24

Nijushiho, 58, 62, 172
Nippon Kempo, 39, 50
Niseishi (see Nijushiho)
Nishiyama, Hidetaka, 55, 56, 67, 71, 75, 76, 79, 87, 84, 93, 95-107, 114, 115, 124-133, 135, 144, 146
Noguchi, Hiroshi, 67, 117
Nozaki, Takehiko, 93
nunchaku, 9, 11-13
nunte, 6-8

Obata, Isao, 36, 55, 56, 67, 70, 73, 85, 87, 117
Ochi, Hideo, 115
Odake, Tetsuo, 115
Offut AFB, 55
Ogasawara, Chosei, 36
Ogawa, Shintaro, 26
Ohshima, Tsutomu, 90, 117, 119-121
Ohtsuka, Hironori, 41, 80, 116
Okamoto, Hideki, 115
Okazaki, Teruyuki, v. 67, 79, 81-83, 91-93, 110, 111, 115, 118, 124, 125, 127, 132-133, 136, 139, 146, 148-149
Okinawa Times newspaper, 36
Okinawa-ken Middle School, 26
Okinawa-te, 4, 5, 13
Okinawan Martial Spirit Promotion Society (see Shobukai)

Okuda, Taketo, 115
Okuyama, 61
Old-Boys Clubs, 62-63, 67, 68, 70, 72, 73, 74, 117-118
Olympics, 101, 112
one-step sparring (see kihon-ippon kumite)
Onishi, Eizo, 86, 90
Orito, Hiroshi, 90
Osaka, Japan, 39, 61, 69, 78
Outer Mongolia, 64
Oyadomari, 171
Oyama, Masutatsu, 88
Otis, Edmond, 97, 146, 147, 148
Ozawa, Osamu, v., 69-70, 147, 150-163

Pai, 66
Pan American Karate Union (PAKU), 114, 129
Passai (see Bassai Dai/Bassai Sho)
Patasai (see Bassai Dai/Bassai Sho)
Patterson, Cecil, 90
Pearl Harbor, 53
Peking, China, 64, 66
Philippines, the, 83, 115
Pinan (see Heian kata)
Prefectural Agricultural School, 26
Prefectural Daiichi Middle School, 26
Prefectural Fisheries School, 26

Readers Digest, 80
Reilly, Robin, 95
Rentan Goshin Karate-jutsu (see Ryukyu Kempo: Karate
Rhee, Jhoon, 90
Rohai (see Meikyo)
Ryobukan (see Shindo-jinen-ryu)
Ryukyu Islands, 1-3
Ryukyu Kempo: Karate, 36-37

SAC (see Strategic Air Command)
Safar, Leslie, 95, 111, 133, 134, 138, 139, 147, 148
Sagara, Juichi, 115
sai, 6-8, 9
Saigo, Kichinosuge, 47, 70
Sainei-Kan hall, 38
Sakugawa, "Tode," 6
samurai, 23, 75, 143, 153
Sanaeda, 172
Sanchin, 15, 61
Sanseryu, 37
Sasaki, Kunio, 115, 116
Sasaki, Yasuyuki, 115
sashi, 17, 19
Satsuma Domain, 3
Sawayama, Muneomi, 39
Schmidt, Stan, 116, 117, 118
Seichin (see Hangetsu)
Seishan, 37
Shikoku, Japan, 85
Shimazu clan, 3-4

Shindo-jinen-ryu, 42, 116
Shiofu (see Wankan)
Shirai, Hiroshi, 95, 115, 117
Shito-ryu, 27, 39, 40, 42, 61, 62, 78, 80, 91, 99, 171, 172, 173, 184
Shizoku class, 23
Sho family, 34
Sho, Hashi, 3
Sho, Shin, 3
Shobukai, 29-30
Shodai University, 39
Shokyo (see Ji'in)
Shorei, 15
Shoreiji-ryu, 15
Shorin, 15, 61
Shorinji-Kempo, 85
Shotai, 34
Shoto Niju Kun (Shoto's 20 Precepts), 164-166
Shoto-kai, 118-121
Shotokan Karate International, 117, 132, 146
Shotokan Karate of America, 90, 117
Shotokan, the (Shotokan dojo), 48
Shotokan Tiger, 51
shu-ha-ri, 23
Shudokan, 41
Shukokai, 86
Shuri Castle, 28-29
Shuri, Okinawa, 23, 26
Shuri-te, 41
Shurijijo Elementary School, 26

Siam, 3
Sifu, 65, 66
SKI (see Shotokan Karate International)
Smith, Frank, 95, 97, 100, 111
So, Doshin, 85
Sochin, 37, 61, 174
Society for Research in High School Physical Education, 35
sport karate, 26-27, 59, 73-77
Sports Illustrated magazine, 135
Strategic Air Command, 54-56, 80, 85-89
Sueyoshi, Bakumonto, 36
Sugimura, Koichi, 115
Sugiura, Motokuni, 67, 78, 145
Sugiura, Toshio, 92, 125
Sugiyama, Shojiro, 93-94, 124
Suidobata, 36
Sumatra, 3
Suparinpei, 37
suruchin, 13

T'ang (see kara)
T'ang Dynasty, 14
Tabata Poplar Club, 35, 51
tachi, 2
Tachikawa AFB, 85
Tae Kwon Do, 90
Tai Chi, 65
taiho-jutsu, 86
Taikyoku kata, 119-120
Taira clan, 2
Tairamachi, 25
Takagi, Masatomo, 67, 68, 70, 72, 80, 129
Takahara, Peichin, 6
Takahashi, Gene, 99, 100
Takahashi, George, 100
Takashina, Shigeru, 94, 115, 127, 128, 150
Takushoku University (Takudai), 39, 55, 63, 67, 68, 72
Tanaka, Masahiko, 138
Tanaka, Noriaki, 82
Tanaka, Yasutaka, 115
Tani, Chojiro, 86
te, 3-4, 13
te gua, 6-13
Tekki kata, 34, 58, 169, 174, 175
Ten-no-kata, 119-120
Tensho, 61
tetsugeta, 16-17, 19
Thai boxing, 83
Thailand, 81
to-hai, 13
Tode, 14
Tokashiki, 24
Tokorozawa AFB, 85
Tokyo Bar Association, 35, 45
Tokyo Civic Center, 45
Tokyo Department Store, 38
Tokyo Invitational Prize Contest for Athletes, 38
Tokyo Metropolitan Gymnasium, 77

Tokyo *Nichinichi* newspaper, 36
Tokyo Railroad Company, 38
Tokyo Shoka Daigaku, 34
Tokyo University karate club, 39
Tomari-te, 170, 173
Tomiki, Kenji, 55
Tominakoshi, Gisu, 23
tonfa, 9, 11
Tono, Norihiro, 36
Toono, 24
Toshima, 48
Toyama, Kanken, 41, 85, 171
Traditional Karate Tournament International, 147, 158
Trias, Robert, 90
Tulleners, Tonny, 97, 111

U.S. Chito Kai, 91
U.S.-Japan Collegiate Tournament, 100
U.S.-Japan Goodwill Karate Tournament, 101
Uechi-ryu, 90
United States Air Force, 85
Unsu, 37, 58, 174
Urban, Peter, 90
Uriu, Sadaru, 115
Useshi (see Gojushiho)

Wado-ryu, 41, 42, 90, 116, 170, 172, 182
Wandau, 37
Wando, 37
Wankan, 175
Wankuan, 37
Wanshu (see Empi)
Waseda University, 55, 67, 68, 72, 90, 117-120
Watanabe, Toshiro (see Kamata, Toshiro)
Way of Karate Beyond Technique, The, 117-118
White, Paul, 100
wing chun dummy, 18
Women's Higher Normal School, 31
World Karate Championship Tournament, 101, 105, 108-109, 111-113
World Union of Karate-do Organizations (WUKO) 99, 101, 107, 109-114
Yabe, James, 95, 98, 111, 126, 142
Yabu, Kentsu, 28
Yaguchi, Yutaka, 82, 93, 100, 115, 127, 129, 150
Yahiku, Moden, 27
Yamaguchi, Gogen, 15, 40, 80, 86, 88, 90
yari, 2
Yashiro, Rokuro, 36
Yokosuka AFB, 85
Yotsuya dojo, 68, 121
yumi, 2

Zen, 50
Zen Buddhists, 14
Zoshigaya, 48